STYLE STUDIES *in* ANITA DESAI

STYLE STUDIES *in* ANITA DESAI

M. CHAKRANARAYAN

ATLANTIC PUBLISHERS AND DISTRIBUTORS

Published by
ATLANTIC PUBLISHERS AND DISTRIBUTORS
B-2, Vishal Enclave, Opp. Rajouri Garden, New Delhi-27
Phones : 5413460, 5429987
Web : www.atlanticbooks.com
e-mail : info@atlantibooks.com

Sales Office
4215/1, Ansari Road, Darya Ganj, New Delhi-110 002
Phones : 3273880, 3285873, 3280451
Fax : 91-11-3285873

ISBN 81-7156-910-2

Typeset at
APD Computer Graphics, Delhi
Printed in India at
Mehra Offset Press, Delhi

Preface

This book is an outcome of an impelling quest for independent and objective methods of literary judgement. As a teacher, I always felt the need for an objective basis for forming critical opinion of texts. Accepting unsubstantiated opinion was difficult for me. I always feel that learning and teaching are steps towards self-realisation and as such can only be satisfactory if they result in the joy of discovery. Stylistic analysis of texts, supported by critical theory and proven opinion has fulfilled this long felt need. Close study of texts based on verifiable data lends an insight and understanding which is both revealing and rewarding. It redeems the appreciation of literary texts from abstract terminology and cliché ridden expression often signifying nothing. Stylistics does not aim merely at the classification of data. If goes much further by disclosing the hidden meaning which often escapes impressionistic observations.

These style studies in Anita Desai have yielded more than satisfactory results. The inner drama of human psyche can be one of the most engrossing subjects, as it helps us to understand ourselves.

My interest in stylistics is the result of the Post-Graduate Diploma in the Teaching in English offered by the Central Institute of English and Foreign Languages, Hyderabad. The lectures on educational psychology, delivered by my esteemed Professor D.G. Kasture, have also been of immense help in gaining insight into the subject.

In the publication of this book, my special thanks are due to Dr. (Smt.) Vijaya Chouhan, who has been the main source of inspiration and guidance to me. I am also indebted to my colleagues in the department, especially to Dr. S.B. Shrivastava,

Prof. M.J. Pinto, Late Prof. D.K. Moitra, Dr. S. Banerjee, Dr. S. Nair and Dr. Usha Bande. I gratefully acknowledge the computer assistance of Dr. D.K. Pandey, Deptt. of Physics, R.D.V.V., Jabalpur.

In the end, I fondly include my husband Prof. V. Chakranarayan and my sons Ashish and Vishwas, who have kept me buoyed in my journey of life. The journey which I started with my mother Florence C. Gill, who gave me the watch-word 'Courage' and who taught me these famous lines of H.W. Longfellow :

Life is real, life is earnest,
And the grave is not its goal,
Dust thou art, to dust returnest,
Was not spoken of the soul.

M. CHAKRANARAYAN

CONTENTS

1

INTRODUCTION

The musical novels of Anita Desai with their plaintive numbers have captivated many a reader and scholar. Her eight novels, *Cry the Peacock* (1963), *Voices in the City* (1965), *Bye-Bye Black Bird* (1971), *Where Shall We Go This Summer*? (1975), *Fire on the Mountain* (1977), *Clear Light of Day* (1980), *The Village by the Sea* (1982), and *In Custody* (1984), sing the eternal song of human woe and misery and also the release which the soul experiences in a moment of awakening.

Anita Desai has evoked mixed response from her readers. Some have acclaimed her as a great artist, whose 'writings reveal inner realities and psychic reverberations of her characters'.[1] A writer whose forte is the exploration of sensibility "that lours or clears or rumbles like thunder or suddenly blazes forth like lightning, is more compelling than the outer weather, the physical geography or the visible action".[2] Others have declaimed her as a writer who is "unable to invent events and episodes that may bring out the dramatic potential in her novels, there are therefore no great scenes in her, but moments of lyric beauty and intensity".[3] Her prose, which has won praise even from westerners, has been decried in the following words : "About the use of Desai's English prose style in her novels, one may sadly remark that she found it marble but left it stone".[4] Meenakshi Mukerjee remarks about Anita Desai, "Her language is marked by three characteristics : sensuous richness, a high-strung sensitiveness, and a love of sound of words".[5] On the other hand Shiv K. Kumar writes, "Never does the writer relax her grip on the style which often freezes into a strange academic anaemia, stilted and petrified, it abounds in tritely compounded and palpably alliterative passages".[6]

A controversial figure always evokes curiosity and the present study is an attempt to objectively evaluate the existing conflicting opinions about Anita Desai.

This is possible by a close study of the text. It has been rightly remarked that :

> "A writer's style may be regarded as an individual and creative utilization of the resources of language, which his period, his chosen dialect, his genre, and his purpose within it offer him. To understand and to make explicit his linguistic creativity, to appreciate in full the alchemy by which he transmutes the base metal of everyday language into the gold of art, it is first necessary to recognise and where possible to specify the ranges of language within which he is working, and upon which he is able to draw. The attempt to do so in analytical detail is not to destroy the wonder of literature but to enhance it".[7]

The above words of John Spencer, echo the contemporary belief that linguistics is a contributory force in literary criticism and as such "it is entitled to a place in the baggage of the literary critic as history, biography, bibliography, or psychology — all disciplines which contribute new facts, new ways of looking at facts, and new kinds of theoretical commitments to the craft of studying, explaining and evaluating literary art. Linguistics gives literary criticism a theoretical underpinning as necessary to that undertaking as mathematics is to physics. A good critic is perforce a good linguist".[8]

Stylistics as a branch of linguistics and a "handmaid to literary criticism" is gradually gaining ground. The objective medium and the ensuing insight into a piece of literature is a gratifying experience for the researcher. Paradoxically, although depending on purely verifiable data, the stylistic approach leads to revealing aspects of structure, narrative voice, tone and point of view, which are generally considered as subjective and unamenable to dissections of a linguist. The end product is not merely a study of words, phrases and structures, but the work of art viewed as a unified whole, the understanding of which is aided through the recognition of individual parts and their function. This microcosmic approach helps in better appreciation of the macrocosm of the whole entity and far from limiting the insight to isolated factors, presents a comprehensive view of life itself, the stuff literature is made of.

Linguistic analysis of novels poses certain challenges. A detailed textural analysis of the eight novels of Anita Desai is followed by a study of form, structure and rhetoric of the four major novels. "A novel is a fictional discourse that is in the Aristotlean formulation, necessarily of a certain magnitude and hence of the necessary range of the novel — the problems that derive from our inability to possess a novel as a picture or a lyric can be possessed, seem fundamental".[9] David Lodge[10] suggests two ways of linguistic criticism of novels, (i) textural, *i.e.*, to isolate, deliberately or at random, one or more passages and submit them to close and exhaustive analysis and (ii) structural, *i.e.*, to trace significant threads through the language of an entire novel. Close study of texts can never be wholly representative of a novel but can often yield valuable critical insights'. For textural analysis, approximately the first five hundred words of each novel are taken as sample. The method adopted includes close attention to lexis, grammar, syntax, schemes and tropes, context and cohesion. With regard to style markers, the present study has taken direction from the work of Geoffrey N. Leech and Michael H. Short in their book, *Style in Fiction* (London : Longman, 1981). Care was taken to refrain from the critical material available on Anita Desai till the initial study was over. However, it was astonishing to discover that the findings coincided with most of the prevailing criticism of the works of Anita Desai with the additional advantage of being objectively based.

A global study of the four major novels, *Cry the Peacock*, *Voices in the City*, *Fire on the Mountain*, and *Where Shall We Go This Summer?*, is the subject matter of the next chapter. Edwin Muir says, 'The plot of the novel is as necessarily poetic or aesthetic as that of any other kind of imaginative creation',[11] and this is particularly true of Anita Desai. In this connection Darshan Singh Maini writes,

> "There is, for instance, a type of novel — the lyric novel — which exhibits the state or condition in particular where it succeeds as in Virginia Woolf, the triumph is always exotic, nebulous, suspect. This is because such a novel will not stabilize into a type. It will keep striving for the condition of poetry and music, and will depend, almost tragically on the power of rhetoric. Anita Desai appears to me an example of this aesthetic dilemma. A beautiful and subtle poetic imagination is still struggling to bend, if not subvert a genre for its own purposes".[12]

The lyrical quality of the prose of Anita Desai is apparent to the most casual reader. Based on this impression, an attempt has been made to assess the four novels as lyrical novels. Incidentally, the characteristic features of a lyrical novel, also happen to be those of a 'modern' novel.

Edward Stankiewicz suggests : "In poetic discourse, in which the transmission of information is secondary to the manner of presentation, content itself is defined and limited by the formal organization of the message"...lyric poetry has no thematic or temporal limitations.... . The participants of the speech event may themselves become the subject matter...in lyrical poetry which hinges on the poet himself, that is a fictitious addressor and the emphasis shifts to an imaginary or ubiquitous addressee".[13]

In a lyrical novel the pattern is based on the vision of the poet hero, Maya in *Cry the Peacock*,[14] Nirode, Monisha and Amla, in *Voices in the City*,[15] Nanda Kaul, in *Fire on the Mountain*,[16] and Sita in *Where Shall We Go This Summer*?,[17] all represent the symbolic vision of the poet-narrator. Ralph Freedman in his book 'The lyrical Novel', writes :

> "A decisive difference between the two forms, however is the locus of that world In conventional narratives, the outer world is the thing. It is placed beyond both writer and reader, imposing between them and the theme. In lyrical mode such a world is conceived not as a universe in which men display their actions, but as a

> poet's vision fashioned as a design. The world is reduced to a lyrical point of view, the equivalent of a poet's 'I', the lyrical self. In the masquerade of the novel this point of view is the poet's mask as well as the source of his consciousness, whether it appears as one or more disguised personae or in the more direct function of the diarist, the confessor or first person narrator".[18]

Form and structure are thus an integral part of the study of the style of modern fiction.

In the words of William Van O'Connor "The form, a symbolic structure is not a transcript of life; it is a representation which equips us to understand more fully, aspects of existence outside of art. Form is the objectifying of idea, and its excellence it would seem, depends on its appropriateness to the idea".[19]

The four novels of Anita Desai under consideration for study of form and structure yielded interesting results, and the moment of revelation especially exultant, as David Lodge puts it :

> "The moment of perceiving the pattern is sudden and unexpected. All the time one has been making the tiny provisional notes, measuring each against one's developing awareness of the whole, storing them up in the blind hope that they will prove useful, and then suddenly one such small local observation sends a shock like an electric charge through all the discrete observations heaped up on all sides, so that with an exciting clatter and rattle they fly about and arrange themselves in a certain meaningful order".[20]

Rhetoric plays an important role in a lyrical novel and therefore, the next division of this study deals with fictional sequencing, discourse and discourse situation, types of narration, narrative voice, tone and point of view, with the assumption that linguistic components in a novel contribute towards the total effect of the work. As Jan Mukarovsky observes,

> "It cannot be said of novel, that here the linguistic elements are the aesthetically indifferent expression of content, not even if they appear to be completely devoid of foregrounding, the structure is the total of all the components, and its dynamics arises precisely from the tension between the foregrounded and unforegrounded components. In the arts we evaluate each component in

terms of the structure of the work in question, and the yardstick is in each individual case determined by the function of the component within the structure".[21]

In the opinion of Wayne Booth, "Rhetoric is the technique of non-didactic fiction viewed as the art of communicating with the readers".[22] Leech and Short also express the same idea, in their book, *Style in Fiction* "Rhetoric is used here in the traditional sense of the 'art or skill' of effective communication".[23]

"The following dimensions can be singled out in any linguistic utterance : (1) the subject matter, that is the thing spoken about, the referent, or the semantic dimension; (2) the participants — speaker and addressee; (3) the speech act, that is the concrete physical event, the delivery of the message; (4) the code, that is the language in which the message is transmitted and (5) the message".[24] The first and fourth dimensions listed above are discussed in Chapter 2 and 3 of this study. The remaining three dimensions are covered under the term 'rhetoric'. The units of discourse and discourse situation, speech and thought presentation, types of narration, narrative voice and tone explicate the second and third dimensions, while fictional sequencing and point of view do the same for the fifth dimension.

Enkvist observes : "Style is one of those areas where linguistics, pragmatics and aesthetics readily overlap. Part of the difficulty in discussing style follows from the temptation to attempt simultaneous answers to linguistic, pragmatic and aesthetic question".[25]

The present study, as far as possible focuses on descriptive linguistic features that occur in a given text and on analysis of their distribution and frequency. "Literary stylistics deals with rather different problems and has begun to devise its own methods for attacking them. Here, too, there are two main possibilities : we may proceed either by direct observation or on a numerical basis".[26] Professor Leo Spitzer is the chief exponent of direct method of observation, which is also known as 'psychological stylistics', because of its strong emphasis on connections between an author's mental make up and his language. The procedure of indirect observation is called the 'philological circle' by Spitzer.

"The philological circle is an operation with three distinct phases. In the first phase, the student will merely read and reread the text and allow it to act on him until he is struck by some persistently recurrent peculiarity, a type of imagery, a syntactical construction, a rhythmic pattern or any other feature. Next he will try to relate this stylistic trait to some element in the author's psyche. In the third place, he will make the return journey from the centre to the periphery and will look for further manifestations, linguistic or otherwise of the same mental feature".[27]

The method followed in the present study is mainly that of direct observation, supplemented by numerical data. However, no claim is made to the precision of the numerical evidence, as only a rough indication of frequencies was considered essential for the needs of the work in hand. To quote Ullman again : "Numerical data is not considered an end in themselves, they are merely the first step towards what remains the principal task of stylistics : a qualitative interpretation of the facts of style".[28]

REFERENCES

1. Usha Bande, *The Novels of Anita Desai* (New Delhi : Prestige Books, 1988), p. 7.
2. K.R. Shrinivas Iyengar, *Indian Writing in English* (1962; rpt. New Delhi : Sterling Publishers, 1983), p. 464.
3. Darshan Singh Maini, "Anita Desai's Novels : An Evaluation, in *Perspectives on Anita Desai*", ed. R.K. Shrivastava (Ghaziabad : Vimal Prakashan, 1984), p. 136.
4. F.A. Inamdar, "Anita Desai's Prose Style," in *Perspectives on Anita Desai*, p. 102.
5. Meenakshi Mukerjee, *Twice Born Fiction* (New Delhi : Arnold Heinmann, 1974), p. 189.
6. Shiv, K. Kumar, "Art and Experience : A note on Anita Desai as a short story writer", in *The Twofold Voice* : Essay in honour of Ramesh Mohan, ed. Rizvi. (Austria : Institute fur Anglistik and Amerikanastik, 1982), pp. 191-92.
7. John Spencer, Preface, *Linguistics and Style : Nils Erik Enkvist, John Spencer, Michael Gregory*, ed. John Spencer (London : Oxford University Press, 1964).
8. Donald C. Freeman, *Linguistics and Literary Style* (New York : Holt Rinchart and Winston Inc., 1970), p. 3.

9. Mark Spilka, *Towards a Poetics of Fiction* (Bloomington and London : Indiana University, 1977), p. 7.
10. David Lodge, *Language of Fiction* (London : Routledge and Kegan Paul, 1966), pp. 78-79.
11. Quoted from, WJM Brorzwaer, *Tense in the Novel* (Wolters, the Netherlands : Noordhoff Publishing Groningen, 1970), p. 1.
12. Darshan Singh Maini in *Perspectives on Anita Desai*, p. 118.
13. Edward Stankiewicz, "Linguistics and the study of Poetic Language", in *Style in Language*, ed. T.A. Sebeok (New York : The Technology Press of Massachusetts, 1960), p. 73.
14. Anita Desai, *Cry the Peacock* (1963; rpt., Delhi : Vision Books, 1983).
15. Anita Desai, *Voices in the City* (1965; rpt., New Delhi : Orient Paperbacks, 1982).
16. Anita Desai, *Fire on the Mountain* (1977; rpt., Middlesex : Penguin, 1984).
17. Anita Desai, *Where Shall We Go This Summer*? (Delhi : Orient Paperbacks, 1975).
18. Ralph Freedman, p. 8.
19. William Van O'Connor, *Forms of Modern Fiction* (1959; rpt., Bloomington : Indiana Univ. Press, 1964), p. 3.
20. David Lodge, p. 81.
21. Jan Mukarovsky, "Standard Language and Poetic Language", in *Linguistics and Literary Style*, ed. D.C. Freeman, pp. 48-49.
22. Wayne C. Booth, *The Rhetoric of Fiction* (Chicago : University Press, 1961), Preface.
23. Geoffery N. Leech and Michael H. Short, *Style in Fiction* (London : Longman, 1981), p. 210.
24. Edward Stankiewicz, in *Style in Language*, p. 71.
25. Nils Erik Enkvist, "On Defining style, in *Linguistics and Style*, p. 47.
26. Stephen Ullman, *Style in French Novel* (Oxford : Basil Blackwell, 1964), p. 27.
27. *Ibid.*, p. 27.
28. *Ibid.*, pp. 30-31.

★★★

2

THE MAGIC OF A PAGE

> 'How often, with all the theoretical experience of method accumulated in me over the years have I stared blankly, quite similar to one of my beginning students, at a page that would not yield it's magic. The only way out of this state of unproductivity is to read and reread'.[1]
>
> —*Leo Spitzer*

The magic of a page is what stylistics tries to unravel. The beautiful structures of literature are made of words in all their different forms. The quality and quantity of words used, determine the overall utility and aesthetic value of any piece of writing.

Stylistics aims at analysing this very fundamental stuff of which literature is made. To establish the strength and beauty of literary writings, stylistics tries to probe deep into the meaning of structures. As Leech and Short put it : 'Stylistics tries to explore for pattern and system below the surface forms of language, to search for principles of meaning and language use, which activate and control the code'.[2]

Stylisticians believe that style is a matter of choice. Every writer has his own peculiar choice of words and structures which make his writings unique. Modern stylistics focuses on these particular choices of the writer in order to understand the underlying pattern.

J. Warburg in his article 'Some Aspects of Style', propounded a theory of value in which he writes,

> 'The good use of a language, then, consists in choosing the appropriate symbolisation of the experience you wish to convey, from among all possible words and arrangements of words (by saying, for example, dog

> rather than cat)'. 'Good style, it seems to me, consists in choosing the appropriate symbolisation of the experience you wish to convey, from among a number of words whose meaning area is roughly, but only roughly, the same (by saying cat, for example, rather than pussy). That is to say, matters of style are necessarily linguistic matters : linguistic matters are not necessarily — it is a common but misleading view — matters of style.'[3]

The function of literary stylistics is to explain the relation between language and artistic function. The motivating questions are not so much 'what' but 'why' and 'how'.

Why a particular writer chooses the words phrases, and structures for his works and how he uses them to achieve the result is the main enquiry of stylistics.

The methods adopted for the above purpose acknowledge both ends of the scale *i.e.*, aesthetic and linguistic. Sometimes it is assumed that the task of stylistics is to provide a hard and fast technology of analysis. That is not the case. "There is a cyclic motion whereby linguistic observation stimulates or modifies literacy insight, and whereby literacy insight in its turn stimulates further linguistic observation. This notion is something like the cycle of theory formulation and theory testing! which underlies scientific method".[4]

It has been rightly said : 'Stylistics is not a mechanical technique of style analysis. It acknowledges that intuition and personal judgement of the reader cannot be replaced by any method. The mystery of having been moved by words as Dylan Thomas says, will always remain'.[5]

Of course, one major task of stylistics is to check and validate intuitions by detailed analysis. For this purpose, objective methods of analysis are employed. A detailed analysis of a prose piece will include careful study of the lexis, grammar, the schemes and tropes, cohesive and contextual devices, but the end is not mere objectivity but insight into the work of art.

"Linguistic analysis does not replace the reader's intuition, what Spitzer calls 'the click in the mind' : but it may prompt, direct and shape it into an understanding".[6]

The quantitative selection of data has its own advantage over the subjective methods of discussing style. It has two functions. First to substantiate the observations based on insight and second to be a ready proof in case those observations are challenged. However point to point mathematical accuracy is not the aim. A rough indication of frequencies is generally a good guide to objective study of style.

"In the study of prose fiction, character, theme, and argument are generally considered more important, but the great artists have always acknowledged the place of verbal artistry in the overall artistic achievement of their work. As Flaubert remarks : 'You say that I pay too much attention to form. Alas! it is like body and soul : form and content to me are one. I don't know what either is without the other. The finer the idea, be sure, the finer sounding the sentence. The exactness of the thought makes for (and is itself), that of the word'."[7]

The vastness of prose fiction poses certain problems for minute style analysis. Hence an analysis of a full scale novel, if not impossible, is not an easily manageable task. As David Lodge observes :

> 'All novel criticism is carried out in the teeth of methodological difficulties which seem to press particularly hard on criticism concerned with the language of the novel. I refer to the fact first explicitly formulated, perhaps by Percy Lubbock, that novels are such vast and complicated structures, and our experience of them is so extended in time that it is impossible for the human mind to conceive of a novel as a whole without blurring or forgetting the parts through the accumulation of which this totality has been conveyed.'[8]

According to Lodge, a novel critic can either isolate deliberately or at random, one or more passages and submit them to close exhaustive analysis, or trace significant threads through the language of an entire novel.

"The first may be termed as the textural approach and the second structural. Textural criticism probably works most satisfactorily on the beginnings of the novels, as they are the only independent units in novels, since nothing else precedes them. Leech and Short also agree with this : 'A point of particular concentration is the beginning of the fiction, which, according to the principle above, ought to be the point of least pre-supposition'.[9]

A structural approach attempts to take into account the linguistic character of the whole work. Both the approaches have their own limitations. The great local variation of tone and verbal intensity makes it very difficult to subject a whole novel to exhaustive stylistic analysis. As it is observed : "The analysis of a great novel suffers from bittiness",[10] *i.e.*, at best the stylistic analysis of a novel can only be in bits and pieces.

Style Markers and their Stylistic Indications

An attempt has been made in the present study to synthesize the two methods of analysis mentioned above.

A detailed textural analysis has been carried out of approximately 500 words of the beginnings of the eight novels of Anita Desai. Studies based on the structural approach include the lyrical element and rhetoric of the novels.

In order to carry out the textural analysis, a few style markers have been selected, as in any practicable stylistic analysis, it is essential to decide upon a definite line of study. However, these markers are a general guide to the analysis. Each novel of Anita Desai seems to offer something unique, and as such, emphasis on particular markers, differs from novel to novel.

A. Checklist of Linguistic and Stylistic Categories[11]

(i) *General* : Is the vocabulary simple or complex? (Number of syllables in each word.) Formal or colloquial? Descriptive or evaluative? General or specific? How far does the writer make use of the emotive or other associations of words, as opposed to their referential meaning? Does the text contain idiomatic phrases? If so, what kind of dialect or register, are these idioms associated? Is there any use of rare or specialized vocabulary? Are any particular morphological categories noteworthy (*e.g.*, compound words, words with particular suffixes)? To what semantic fields do words belong?

(ii) *Nouns* : Are the nouns abstract or concrete? What kinds of abstract nouns occur, *e.g.*, nouns referring to events, perceptions, processes, moral qualities, social qualities ? What use is made of proper names? Collective nouns? Collocations.

(iii) *Adjectives* : Are the adjectives frequent? To what kinds of attributes do adjectives refer? physical, psychological? visual? auditory? colour? referential? emotive? evaluative? etc. Are adjectives restrictive or non-restrictive? gradable or non-gradable? attributive or predicative?

(iv) *Verbs* : Do the verbs carry an important part of the meaning? Are they stative (referring to states), or referring to actions, events, etc.? Do they refer to movements, physical acts, speech acts, psychological states or activities, perceptions etc.? Are they transitive, intransitive, linking (intensive), etc.? Are they factive or non-factive?

(v) *Adverbs* : Are adverbs frequent? What semantic functions do they perform (manner, place, direction, time, degree etc.)? Is there any significant use of sentence adverbs (conjuncts such as so, therefore, however : disjuncts such as certainly, obviously, frankly)?

B. Grammatical Categories

(i) *Sentence types* : Does the author use only statements (declarative sentences), or does he also use questions, commands, exclamations, or minor sentence types (such as sentences with no verb)? If these other types are used, what is their function?

(ii) *Sentence Complexity* : Do sentences on the whole have a simple or complex structure? What is the average sentence length? (in number of words). What is the ratio of dependent to independent clauses? Does complexity vary strikingly from one sentence to another? Is complexity mainly due to (i) coordination, (ii) subordination, (iii) parataxis (juxtaposition of clauses or other equivalent structures)? In what parts of a sentence does complexity tend to occur? For instance, is there any notable occurrence of anticipatory structure, *e.g.*, of complex subjects preceding the verbs of dependent clauses, preceding the subject of a main clause.

Clause Types : What types of dependent clauses are favoured? relative clauses, adverbial clauses, different types of nominal clauses (that — clauses, wh-clauses, etc.)? Are reduced or non-finite clauses commonly used and if so, of what type are they? (infinitive clauses, -ing clauses, ed-clauses, verbless clauses).

Verb Phrases : Are there any significant departures from the use of simple past tense? Occurrences and functions of the present tense : of the progressive aspect *(e.g.*, was lying); of the perfective aspect (*e.g.*, has/had appeared); of modal auxiliaries (*e.g.*, can, must, would, etc.).

Minor Word Classes : Prepositions, conjunctions, pronouns, determiners, auxiliaries, interjections. Are particular words of these types used for particular effect? (*e.g.*, the definite and indefinite article, first person pronouns, I, We, etc., demonstratives, such as, this and that, negative words, such as, not, nothing, no).

General : Any general types of grammatical construction used for special effect? (*e.g.,* comparative or superlative constructions; coordinative or listing constructions; parenthetical constructions; appended or interpolated structures; such as/occur in casual speech).

C. Figures of Speech

(i) *Grammatical and lexical schemes* : Are there cases of formal and structural repetition (anaphora, parallelism etc.)? Is the rhetorical effect of these one of antithesis, reinforcement, climax, anticlimax, etc.?

(ii) *Phonological schemes* : Are there any phonological patterns of rhyme, alliteration, assonance, etc.? Are there any salient rhythmical patterns? Do vowel and consonant sounds pattern or cluster in particular ways? How do these phonological features interact with meaning?

(iii) *Tropes* : Are there any obvious violations of, or departures from the linguistic code? Are there any neologisms (such as, Americanly)? deviant lexical collocations (such as portentous infants)? semantic, syntactic, phonological or graphological deviations?

D. Context and Cohesion

(i) *Cohesion* : Does the text contain logical or other links between sentences (*e.g.*, coordinating conjunctions, or linking adverbials)? Or does it tend to rely on implicit connections of meaning?

What sort of use is made of cross-reference by pronouns (she, it, they, etc.)? by substitute forms (do, to, etc.), or ellipsis? Alternatively, is any use made of elegant variation.

Are meaning connections reinforced by repetition of words and phrases, or by repeatedly using words from the same semantic field?

(ii) *Context* : Does the writer address the reader directly, or through the words or thoughts of some fictional character? What linguistic clues (*e.g.* first-person pronouns, I, me, my, mine), are there of the addresser-addressee relationship? What attitude does the author imply towards his subject? If a character's words or thoughts are represented, is this done by direct quotation (direct speech), or by some other method (*e.g.* indirect speech, free indirect speech)? Are there significant changes of style according to who is supposedly speaking or thinking the words on the page.

Stylistic Indications of Some of the Categories

Short Sentences : Convey an impression of speed and therefore suited to the narration of action and historical events.[12] (Herbert Read, p. 35).

Long Sentences : suggest deliberation and solemnity. (Herbert Read, p. 35).

Complex sentences : best suited to express complex ideas and feelings. They afford variety shift emphasis and help elaboration. (H. Read, p. 35).

Antithetical sentences : effectively express contrasting ideas. Add point and vivacity. If abused make description tedious and artificial. They also balance two opposite ideas. (H. Read, p. 40).

Anticipatory constituents : bring an element of suspense into the syntax.[13]

Periodic sentence structure : builds a suspense, adds dramatic quality to the writing, and is an effective device for end-focus. (Leech and Short, p. 227).

Parataxis : is associated with simple and naive narration.[14]

Wh-questions : used for seeking new information. (Fowler, p. 114).

Yes or no questions : allow little or no freedom to reply. (Fowler, p. 114).

Tag questions : are demanding, pointedly request confirmation of an assertion made. (Fowler, pp. 114-15).

Rhetorical questions : function as forceful statements. A positive rhetorical question is like a strong negative assertion, while a negative question is like a strong positive one.[15]

Modality : is the grammar of explicit comment, the means by which people express their degree of commitment to the truth of the proposition they utter, and their desirability, or otherwise of the states of affairs referred to. (Fowler, p. 131).

Non-finite clauses : *i.e.* clauses with infinitive with to, infinitive without to, ing-participle, ed-participle are marks of a careful style. They serve the purpose of compression and compactness. If applied indiscriminately they make the writing ambiguous. (Quirk and Greenbaum, p. 311).

Emotive Emphasis : depends on the emphasis given by information, focus and theme. The language also provides means of giving a unit purely emotional emphasis. Exclamations, expletives, intensifiers, including the general clause emphasisers, such as, actually, really, indeed are included. (Quirk and Greenbaum, p. 427).

Copula or linking verbs : intensify verbal complementation. The most common of these verbs are : be, appear, feel (N), look (N), remain (N), seem (N), sound, smell, taste, become (N), get (chiefly informal), go, grow, turn (N), make (N only), etc. (Quirk and Greenbaum, p. 352).

Notional Classes of Metaphor[16]

Certain types of semantic connections which are traditionally recognised as more important than others, include :

(i) *The Concretive Metaphor*, which attributes concreteness or physical existence to an abstraction : 'the pain of separation', 'the light of learning, etc.'.

(ii) *The Animistic Metaphor*, which attributes animate characteristics to the inanimate : 'an angry sky', 'graves yawned', 'killing half-an-hour', etc.

(iii) *The Humanizing* ('*Anthropomorphic*') *Metaphor*, which attributes characteristics of humanity to what is not human : 'This friendly river', 'laughing valleys', etc.

(iv) *The Synaesthetic Metaphor*, which transfers meaning from one domain of sensory perception to another : 'Warm colour', 'dull sound', 'loud perfume', etc.

Textural Analysis of the Beginning Pages of the Eight Novels of Anita Desai

CRY THE PEACOCK[17] (Novel I)

Text from *Cry the Peacock*

All day the body lay rotting in the sun (1). It could not be moved on to the verandah for, in that April heat, the reek of dead flesh was overpowering and would soon have penetrated the rooms (2). So she moved the little string bed on which it lay under the lime trees, where there was a cool, aqueous shade, saw its eyes open and staring still, screamed and rushed to the garden tap to wash the vision from her eyes, continued to cry and ran, defeated, into the house (3). The gardener came and drew its eyelids down with two horny thumbs reflectively sad as when he laid a dead branch that he had to cut off, on the compost heap (4). But he would not bury it, as she begged him to do (5). Often in the course of that day he said to her, patiently, 'The sweeper will do it (6). He has gone to visit his brother, but when he returns he will do it' (7). It was afternoon now, and the sweeper had not returned (8). Crows sat in a circle around the corpse, and crows will eat anything — entrails, eyes, anything (9). Flies began to hum amidst the limes, driving away the gentle bees and the unthinking butterflies (10). She thought she saw the evil glint of a bluebottle, and grew hysterical (11). The gardener sent his wife to take her into the house and keep her there (12). She sat there, sobbing, and waiting for her husband to come home (13). Now and then she went out onto the verandah, and looked to see if he were coming up the drive which lay shrivelling, melting and then shrivelling again, like molten lead in a groove cut into the earth, and, out of the corner of her eye, could not help glancing, as one cannot help a tic, at the small white corpse laying at one end of the lawn, under a sheet, under the limes (14).

Later in the evening, when the sun hung pendent from the topmost branches of the trees, swelling visibly like — she thought — a purulent boil, until it was ripe to drop, her husband came home (15). He was very late (16). But as soon as he came, he did all that was to be done, quickly and quietly like a surgeon's knife at work (17). He telephoned the Public Works Department, he had them send their scavenging truck to take the corpse away, and saw to it himself that they lifted it in with care (18). 'Yes, yes, the bed too,' he said (19). 'By all means, burn it too' (20). When the truck had left, he came to her, wiping his fingers on a handkerchief much used and soiled during the day, yet still in neat folds (21). 'It is all over,' he said (22). 'Come and drink your tea, and stop crying. You mustn't cry' (23).

But she would not lift her face from a cushion, for fear the stench of decaying flesh still hung in the bougainvillaea coloured evening air (24). All day it had come in with the slow breeze that sucked the curtains in, then slowly drew them out (25).

Analysis

A woman is seen lamenting over a dead body, which has been shifted to the shade of lime trees, where it is cool and damp. The dead body's eyes were open, the sight of which scares the woman and she screams, rushes to the garden tap to wash her eyes. She continues crying and runs inside the house. The gardener closes the eyes of the dead body with his horny thumbs. The woman urges him to bury the body, but he waits for the sweeper. Crows and even bluebottles circle round the corpse. The woman waits for her husband, watches the drive intently for his arrival, at the same time steals a glance at the dead body covered with a sheet. The hot sun aggravates the reek of dead flesh, and with it the pain of the suffering woman, for whom the sun is like a discharging boil by now. Her husband comes home very late, but disposes the body in a professional manner. He is confident, unmoved, and advises her in a matter of fact tone. She is still disconsolate, fears the stench of the decaying flesh, which had been blown in and out the whole day.

General observations : The vocabulary is simple and formal. It is both descriptive and evaluative. The author makes free use of emotive associations of words. The text does contain idiomatic phrases.

Nouns : There are only five abstract nouns, rest are all concrete and relate to perceptions and processes. Only the visual and olfacto images have abstract nouns.

Proper nouns : Complete absence of proper nouns.

Collocation : Words related to *eye* and *seeing* are prominent in the passage. *Saw its eyes, vision, her eyes, eyelids, eyes, saw, she thought she saw, looked to see,* (*an illusion*-shrivelling, melting, shrivelling) *corner of her eye, could not help glancing, glancing* a tic, swelling *visibly*, (*like, she thought* — comparison of an *object perceived*), *saw* to it himself, stop *crying* (associated with eyes), *don't cry.*

For the *woman, seeing and thinking* go hand in hand. *She sees, she thinks, she reacts*, cannot help seeing, but this seeing is distorted, illusory. She is helpless in controlling her seeing.

Her *husband*, not only sees but acts with responsibility, and has confidence. He tells her not to cry, implying, stop troubling the eyes and heart about it. He insists on it. *You mustn't cry.* (Sent. 23). For him the end of crying is the end of sorrow.

Adjectives : are frequently used. They are non-gradable, like, *April heat, Compost heap, surgeon's knife, bougainvillaea coloured evening air*, and physical, *i.e.*, gradable. Here Denominal adjectives, denote provenance or style (Quirk and Greenbaum, p. 403).

Adjectives are foregrounded in the passage, as they point to the three different outlooks of life depicted in the passage. (i) *The gardener* considers the body, *a dead branch*, (not the whole tree), closes the eyelids with his *horny thumbs*, considers the situation, as a dead branch on *a compost heap*. Compost heap implies something which generates fertility, although made of death and decay. The gardener takes the event as an integral phase of the cycle of life.

The woman moves the *little* string bed (emotive), under the *cool aqueous* shade (emotive), becomes *hysterical* (psychological), thinks of *gentle* bees, *unthinking* butterflies, the *evil glint* of a bluebottle, *molten* lead, *purulent* boil (indicating imagination and hallucination), *decaying*, *bougainvillaea coloured* evening air (sensitive to colour and smell). For her, the basis of life is feelings, heart, liver and spleen, as the ancients might call it.

The epithets used for the *husband's manner* are, *surgeon's knife*, sends for the *scavenging truck*, *much used and soiled* handkerchief but in *neat* folds. These point to the husband's ability to face the situation objectively. He is deft in his actions, is quick and precise in his decisions, (sends for the scavenging truck, essential for cleaning), his handkerchief is used and soiled, but neatly folded, indicating that, perhaps he over uses things, but in a dignified manner.

Verbs : In this passage carry an important part of the meaning. There is a balance of transitive and intransitive verbs. They refer to movements, physical acts, speech acts and perceptions. Mostly factual in nature, a few of them have emotional connotations. *e.g.*, *screamed*, *defeated*, *begged*, *sobbing* etc.

Adverbs : of place, time and manner are included. Those of manner, give additional information about the characters, *e.g.*, *reflectively*, *patiently* used for the gardener. *Quickly*, *quietly*, used for the husband. *Visibly* (used for the sun), but seen through the consciousness of the woman, slowly (used for the air), is also seen through the woman's consciousness. While the men reveal a patient acceptance, the woman is deluded.

Grammatical Categories

The passage has only four simple sentences, remaining are all complex. Besides declarative sentences a few conversational sentences have also been included. Average sentence length is 20.56 and the ratio of the subordinate clauses to principal clauses is 1:3. Sentences (3, 14 and 15), are the longest in the passage. They all pertain to the woman's reactions, suggesting the complexity of her thoughts.

Parataxis : Sentences (18, 19), indicate the brief authoritative manner of the husband.

Anticipatory clauses : are nine in number. They increase suspense and make the narration dramatic. Complexity of sentences is both due to pre-modification and post-modification.

Short sentences : point to the limited communication between the couple.

Schemes

Metaphors. Horny thumbs, suggesting hard working hands. *Compost heap*, indicating disposal *Gentle bees*, *unthinking butterflies* and *evil glint of bluebottle* are humanizing metaphors, reflecting the woman's sensitiveness. The *sun hung pendent from the topmost branches, swelling visibly, a purulent boil*, until it was *ripe to drop* are synaesthetic metaphors, depicting the delirious thoughts of the woman. *Bougainvillaea coloured evening air*, points to the fact, that, the woman although overwhelmed with grief, is sensitive to the colours and smells around her. *Sucked the curtain in*, hint at the repulsive atmosphere of the place. *Shrivelling, melting* and *shrivelling again* are kinetic images, applied to solid states, a result of the delirious thinking of the woman.

Similes

Like molten lead in a groove cut in the earth, gives the impression of liquidity for something solid & stationary. *As one cannot help a tic*. A tic although insignificant, yet it is discomforting, an apt image to describe the dead pet, *'like a surgeons knife'*, emphasises the quick, sharp, precise but insensitive method of the husband.

Assonance and Alliteration

Crows will eat anything — entrails, eyes, anything.

/Krouz wil i:t *eniØiη* entreilz, aiz *eniØiη*/.

Staring, *still*, *screamed*, also, *shrivelling*, *melting* and *shrivelling* again.

Parallel Construction. Under the sheet, under the limes

Cohesion : The passage describes the reactions of three different persons to a dead body and its disposal. The gardener accepts reality and maintains his composure. He even consoles the woman, but lacks independent action, and hence cannot dispose of the body.

The woman is all nerves, dependent, desolate, hysterical. The husband, confident, controlled and objective. He accepts reality and is also independent in taking decisions and executing them. The gardener consoles, the woman weeps, and the husband acts. This implicit connection of meaning has strong cohesive effects. Besides this, the lexical repetition, pronouns and the definite article (29), have been discreetly added. The use of the definite article, with intangible notions like, *the reek*, the *gentle bees*, *the unthinking* butterflies, *the evil glint* of bluebottle, attaches significance to them which otherwise is denied to them, and point to the sensitive nature of the woman, for whom the world of nature is so much alive.

Context : Although a third person narration, delineating three characters, the passage in reality is an exposition of the consciousness of the woman. The passage begins with the dead body lying in the sun, and the woman's reaction to it, so that she moves the little string bed on which the body lay, under the trees. She is scared to see the open eyes of the dead thing and hence the gardener closes them with his horny thumbs. She begs the gardener to bury it, but he only consoles her. She looks at the insects and birds around the corpse and waits impatiently for her husband. She is almost panicky, when her husband arrives. She finds his actions devoid of all feeling. She is told by him to stop crying, but she is reluctant, as the stench was overpowering the whole day, and it continues to haunts her.

Out of total twentyfive sentences, only eleven refer to the gardener and the husband; the remaining are all about the reactions of the woman. Complete absence of proper nouns, points to the fact, that the author is analysing personality types and not individuals with specific identity. The passage records the reactions of three different temperaments to a single situation.

VOICES IN THE CITY[18] (Novel II)

Text from *Voices in the City*

The train began to pant, as though in preparation for a battle, sending jets of white steam violently into the night sky, and on the platform people loitered in various attitudes of nervousness, impatience and regret, turning now and then to the lights at the head of the platform, waiting for them to change (1). No one ever betrayed reluctance for them to do so except, perhaps, the latecomers pounding along with baggage wobbling and disintegrating on the seemingly hopeless search for the right carriage (2).

'I'm sorry, now, to leave,' Arun reflected (3). He was one of those who never disclosed nervousness or impatience, lounged over a cigarette as though he were relaxing on a terrace at night-fall (4). So it seemed to the red-shirted coolies, the tea-vendors and the stationmaster in grimy white, all stained with the sweat of haste and overwork, but Nirode, casting at him a glance made sly by envy, saw the tautness in the young man's body, and saw how his eyes shone (5).

He threw away his cigarette and immediately lit another (6). 'Liar,' he said (7). 'You're itching to start' (8).

Arun laughed (9). He moved, and from his movement one could see how right Nirode was (10). The man was like a bird poised on the roof's edge for flight, each feather alert and trained for it, vivid in this moment of gigantic expectation (11). He was alight with eagerness (12). Yet he laughed, stammered, 'No, it's not a moment for decisions' (13). I can't decide now what I'd most like to happen... (14).

'I can see that,' Nirode said dryly and flung yet another cigarette down beneath the waiting wheels, immediately drew out another (15). Fortunately they were of the cheapest variety and Arun did not notice (16). They both turned to watch the light unashamedly, breathing with difficulty the acrid air of Howrah station and separation (17).

They could think of nothing else to say and feigned interest instead, in the marriage party at the neighbouring carriage door—the groom in a white sharkskin suit, loaded with garlands of great, odorous marigolds, looking harried and damp, while the bride hid behind a fold in her sequined sari and decorously sniffed (18). Fat jovial men surrounded them, shouting obscene jokes and quaking with laughter at them (19). The women hung back, in a cluster, weeping heart-brokenly for the daughter (20).

'God, look at them,' muttered Nirode, but Arun smiled—he was smiling, his eyes were shining (21). They watched the marriage party till the whistle went and the train began its preliminary lurching, as though it were unused to motion and were practising a bit before the long run (22). There was an uproar amidst the marriage party, and the bride and groom were lifted upon one thrusting wave of obscenity and congratulation up into their carriage (23). Coolies threw bedding-rolls and tiffin-carriers and late-arrivals into carriages that rolled past them, the tea-vendors held out their shirts to receive the last of the copper coins (24). The brothers moved a step closer, but could not look each other in the eye for embarrassment and emotion (25). They shook hands, embraced-later neither could remember his or the other's behaviour at that blurring tearing moment of departure (26).

Analysis

The novel begins with a scene at the busy railway platform of Howrah. The train is about to leave, and Arun and Nirode, two brothers await the moment. Arun is leaving by the train, and Nirode who has come to see him off is envious of his brother's lot. Arun poses to be relaxed, but Nirode knows that he is eager to start a new life in the distant land. Both find the moment of separation difficult, and so try to feign interest in a marriage party, which is leaving by the same train. Nirode is disgusted with the obscene jokes and hypocritical tears of the bride, while Arun is amused. At last the train starts moving, while the workers at the platform mind their mundane business, the marriage party is filled with jubilation, and the brothers embrace and part with each other with mixed emotions.

General observations : Word complexity is higher in this passage compared to the previous one. 161 words out of 516 have more than one syllable. Most of the abstract nouns are polysyllabic. The vocabulary is formal, and includes words of emotive and associative connotations. Idiomatic use of language prevails. A few compound words are included *i.e., tiffin-carriers, late-arrivals, tea-vendors, night-fall, red-shirted, bedding-rolls.*

Nouns : Three proper nouns introduce the two characters, and the locale. Almost equal number of concrete and abstract nouns have been included, but the abstract nouns are foregrounded, as they refer to the mental states of the people at the platform, and that of the protagonists. Many of these abstract nouns have negative connotations *i.e. nervousness, impatience, regret, battle, reluctance, haste*, *over-work*, *envy*, *tautness*, *difficulty*, *separation*, *obscenity*, *embarrassment*. Only three abstract nouns refer to happy states — expectation, eagerness, congratulation. The rest are neutral referring to mental processes and perceptions. Concrete nouns frame the background, essential for balancing the subjective and objective worlds.

Adjectives : refer both to physical and psychological states. To match the nouns with negative connotations, most of the adjectives too have negative implications. Adjectives coupled with abstract nouns, heighten the effect of the unseen mental activity going on in the mind of the protagonists.

Verbs : To match the abstract nouns and adjectives denoting emotive and psychological states and adverbs of negative connotation, verbs mostly intransitive in nature have been included, *viz., loitered*, *pounding*, *wobbling*, *disintegrating*, *reflected*, *lounged*, *relaxing*, *laughed*, *moved*, *seemed*. The transitive verbs equal in number, describe the background activities in the passage, so that the impression of two men watching and observing a scene of hectic activity is pictured vividly.

Adverbs : of manner mostly with negative connotations predominate i.e.; *violently*, *seemingly*, *fortunately*, *unashamedly*, *heartbrokenly*, *dryly*.

Grammatical Categories

Average sentence length is 20.68 words. Only six short sentences of direct speech are included, the rest are all declarative sentences. Sentence no. (1, 2, 5 and 18), are long. Those stating direct speech are the shortest. Complexity is due to subordination and coordination both, but more due to the nature of subordinators, such as : *as though*, *except*, *perhaps*, all are compound subordinators, (Quirk and Greenbaum, p. 292), *but* (3) and yet (2) denoting contrast. Complexity in syntax suggests complexity in ideas. The passage deals more with hidden psychological detail than overt physical surroundings.

Schemes

The train began to pant and *waiting wheels* are both examples of *personification*, the train has been treated as animate, something which signifies journey into the future, symbolising locomotion, uncertainty and promise.

Quasi-simile

As though in preparation for a battle (Sent. 1).

As though he were relaxing on a terrace (Sent. 4).

As though it were unused to motion (Sent. 20).

The above analogies intensify the impression of a mind which constantly tries to analyse and evaluate men and objects around it.

Collocative Clash

Breathing with difficulty, the acrid air of Howrah station and separation. (Sent. 17).

An example of Semantic incompatibility. An olfacto image has been coupled with an abstract quality. The word *separation* is foregrounded. The expression though deviant is very telling, as, just like the *acrid* smell, *separation* is the prevailing feeling on a railway platform and painful too.

Double Negatives

No one ever betrayed reluctance. (Sent. 2).

Seemingly hopeless. (Sent. 2).

The fact that, the objective and the subjective are inseparable, is strengthened by these statements.

Simile

The man *was like a bird poised* on the roof's edge for *flight*, each *feather* alert and trained for it, vivid in this moment of gigantic expectation. He was *alight* with eagerness. (Sent. 11 and 12).

Bird imagery is frequent in the works of Anita Desai. Birds denote nature, flights into fancy and freedom. The epithets used, aptly describe Arun's preparation and expectations.

Assonance and Alliteration

Phonoaesthetic effects are plentiful in the passage. To note a few.

Waiting wheels, *station and separation*, look *each* other in the *eye* for *embarrassment* and *emotion.*

Parenthesis : occurs four times in the passage. It gives an impression of after thought in sentence (1) and (21) and elaboration in sentences (18) and (26).

Cohesion : Paragraph arrangement is conspicuous in the passage. The first paragraph describes the train, ready to leave, in subjective terms, the last also describes the train with objective and subjective elements combined. The middle paragraphs narrate the attitude and reactions of the two brothers. Again the individual is linked to the group by the interest the men show in the marriage party, also by reference to the opinion of the workers at the station about Arun.

Arun's journey by train is compared to the flight of a bird, thus the train serves as a referential link between the sentences and paragraphs. It also serves as a backdrop of palpable world for the mental activity in the forefront.

Context : The passage is a third person narration, containing a commentary on the scene at the railway platform. The focus of attention is two men, Arun and Nirode. In fact, it is Nirode's consciousness which controls the passage. The implicit uncertainty, nervousness, impatience and conflict in Nirode's temperament is made explicit through his interaction with his brother and surroundings. Even though third and fourth paragraphs speak of Arun, it is an interpretation of Nirode's consciousness. The value judgements on the marriage party are also the result of Nirode's sifting of ideas. It is he who is the constant observer, and the remaining world, actors. 'Truth is always in the making,' as Stevenson says, and Nirode trying to see the world with his mind's eye alone, only reaps disappointment.

The passage is in fact, a long metaphor, hinting at the contrasts and contradictions inherent in his character.

Sentence 1.

(i) The train began *to pant* as though in preparation for a *battle.*

(The word *'pant'* suggests gasping for breath. Can a breathless entity be prepared for battle?)

(ii) Sending jets of *white* steam *violently.*

(*white* is the colour of truce, of peace, here it is coupled with *violence.*)

(iii) On the platform people *loitered* in various attitudes of nervousness, impatience and regret.

(*Loitered* suggests passing time indolently, here it is contrasted with attitudes of nervousness, impatience and regret.)

Sentence 2

(iv) No one ever *betrayed reluctance* for them to do so, except perhaps the late comers.

(*Betrayed reluctance*, double negative, makes the sense positive. Explicit contrast, *except*, *perhaps*.)

(v) *Seemingly hopeless* search for the right carriage.

(Again, use of double negatives, implying affirmation, suggesting that finding the right carriage is a matter of chance and choice. It is never too late.)

Sentence 3

(vi) 'I'm sorry, now, to leave', Arun reflected.

(*'now'*, enclosed within two commas hints that Arun is sorry at the prospect of leaving in the present time reference, the idea was welcome to him in the past.

Sentence 4

(vii) He (Arun) was one of those who *never disclosed* nervousness or impatience.

(A contrast between appearance and reality.)

(viii) It *seemed* to the red-shirted coolies, thc tea-vendors etc., that Arun *lounged* over a cigarette, as though *relaxing* on a terrace.

(Actually, Arun felt the opposite.)

Sentence 6

(ix) Nirode *threw away* his cigarette and *immediately lit* another.

(Although not leaving, even Nirode was nervous.)

Sentence 11

(x) The man was like a bird poised on the roof's edge for *flight*, each feather *alert* and trained for it, vivid in this moment of *gigantic expectation*.

(Arun felt the freedom of hope, Nirode was envious. Sent. 5.)

Sentence 15

(xi) Fortunately they were of the cheapest variety and *Arun did not notice.*

(Nirode watches Arun closely, Arun is unmindful of Nirode.)

(xii) They could think of nothing else to say and *feigned interest* instead, in the marriage party.....

(Actually, they were not interested.)

Sentence 19 and 20

(xiii) Fat *jovial* men surrounded them, *shouting* obscene jokes and *quaking with laughter* at them. The women hung back, in a cluster, *weeping heart brokenly* for the daughter.

(The men see the happy side, the physical aspect of marriage, the women see the sad, emotional aspect of it. The use of the word, *daughter* indicates that with reference to female sex.)

Sentence 21

(xiv) 'God, look at them,' *muttered Nirode* but *Arun smiled* — He was *smiling*, his eyes were *shining.*

(Nirode feels disgusted with the scene but Arun is amused. It is a matter of outlook.)

The drama that is enacted in the passage, comprises of three different sets of people. The workers, consumers and thinkers Arun and Nirode belong to the last category. Arun is willing to compromise, and hence he is seen smiling, his shining eyes mean acceptance, whereas Nirode is unwilling to acknowledge and accept the other realities of life, and, therefore, feels frustrated.

BYE-BYE BLACK BIRD[19] (Novel III)

Text from _Bye-Bye Black Bird_

The morning light slid down the lane-lengths of telephone wires, perched a while on the peaks of television aerials and then rolled down the drain pipes into the new-leafed hedges and through the silver caps of the milk bottles on the steps, rang the brass door knockers and set the birds and bottles clinking and clanking in informal good-morning voices that rose up to Dev's window and politely woke him (1). But when he pulled out his watch from under his pillow he was disgusted to find it was barely five o'clock

(2). He wondered if it had died in the night of an inability to acclimatize itself, but its steady ticking asserted itself through the bright bead-curtain of bird-and-bottle sounds and he shoved it away with a groan, then put his head beside it under the pillow (3). But he had mistakenly left the window open at night and now the milky fingers of morning reached through and scrabbled through his winter coverings like a giggling tease and eventually he had to emerge, halfsmothered, from the dark pillow and face the window now swimming with liquid light in which the red roofs and blackened brick walls of Clapham stood steady as the keels and hulls of sound old boats that had weathered the wash and swell of another day's tidal wave (4).

He propped himself up on one elbow, trying to conjure some of yesterday's excitement and buoyancy out of the tiredness of a night's sleep begun too late and ended too early (5). Groping about for the support of a tranquillizing smoke, he found he had left his cigarettes on top of the brass-knobbed dresser at the far end of the room (6). There was nothing for it but to roll out of his dishevelled bed, leap up into the air as his feet touched the freezing floor boards race across to the dresser, snatch up cigarettes and matches and take a flying leap back into his blue quilt (7). Trying nervously to nurse it back to warmth and keep the ashes from falling on the blue satin, he thought with momentary bitterness of the cup of tea that would have been brought to him if he were at home in India now, by a mother fresh from her morning prayers, or a servant boy scorched and sooty from a newly made fire (8). By no stretch of imagination were his host Adit Sen or his wife Sarah likely to do this for him : there was an eiderdown-smothered silence from their end of the flat (9). Once the cigarette had dwindled to a stub and he had to leap up in order to fling it out of the window into the hedge, he felt he might as well wrap his earthen brown shawl about him and go out to find the kitchen and make himself a cup of tea (10). It was the first lesson his first day in London taught him : he who wants tea must get up and make it (11).

Analysis

The morning light mixed with bird voices and milk-bottle sounds, wake Dev on his first day in London. From telephone wires to the door steps, light gradually descends on earth. Dev finds himself uncomfortable in the new surroundings. He had left the window open by mistake, and to ward off the morning cold he will have to leave the bed and shut it. After closing the window, once again in his warm bed, Dev remembers that he had left his cigarettes and lighter on the dresser. With a leap, he reaches the dresser but feels like having a cup of tea, when once again he is inside his quilt. He remembers the routine in India, where his mother or the servant boy would bring him his morning tea. Here in England, he could expect no such comfort. This realisation teaches him his first lesson about life in England. If he wants a cup of tea, he will have to get up and make it.

General Observations

The passage is written in simple idiomatic English. Word complexity is low. Out of 501 words only 132 have more than one syllable. There are many compound words coined by the writer which are foregrounded. *e.g.*, *lane-lengths*, *new-leafed*, *bead-curtain*, *bird and bottle*, *milky-fingers*, *giggling-tease*, *half-smothered*, *brass-knobbed*, *eiderdown-smothered.*

The deviance is both conceptual and non-conceptual. The writer has an individual style which displays freshness, keen observation and insight. The physical as well as the psychological aspects have been intensely felt by the writer.

Nouns

Out of 78 nouns only 15 are abstract in nature. These abstract nouns refer to perceptions and processes both *e.g.*, *voices*, *sounds*, *inability*, *milky fingers*, *giggling-tease*, *excitement*, *buoyancy*, *stretch*, *imagination*, *eiderdown-smothered*, *silence, tiredness*, *bitterness*, *warmth*, *groan*, *wash and swell* etc.

Proper Nouns introduce the reader to the major characters — *Dev*, *Adit*, *Sarah*, the locality and the city — *Clapham*, *London.*

Collocations. Words dealing with marine imagery are prominent. *e.g.*, *swimming*, *liquid*, *tidal wave*, *keels and hulls*, *old boats*, *weathered*, *wash and swell.*

Adjectives and Adverbs. In this passage adjectives and adverbs of manner refer more to the psychological states than physical objects. Since Anita Desai is trying to depict the physical world as apprehended by Dev, who is only one day old in England, these word classes have an important role in describing feelings and reactions. *Excitement*, *buoyancy*, *informal*, *giggling*, *tranquillizing*, *freezing*, *newly*, *politely*, *barely*, *mistakenly*, *nervously*, are all words with emotive connotations. The compound words, *new-leafed*, *bright-bead-curtain*, *bird and bottle sounds*, *giggling tease*, *brass-knobbed*, representing the pleasanter aspect of life in England are juxtaposed with the doubtful bliss of the warm bed, for which epithets like *half-smothered*, *dishevelled*, *eiderdown-smothered*, have been used.

Adverbs of place and direction add movement and dramatic quality to the passage. *Verbs* are very frequent in the passage (58 main verbs). The transitive and intransitive verbs are equal in number. They refer to movements, psychological states and perceptions. The past tense forms have been used with the deictic adverb *now*[20] (Sent. 3 and 8), denoting neither an identifiable present, nor an identifiable past, but a fictive universe outside real time and space. Verbs combined with abstract nouns, adverbs of manner and adjectives with emotive connotation, intensify psychological effects *viz.*, *mistakenly left*, *to conjure excitement and buoyancy*, *groping for support*, *trying nervously*, *leap up*, *pulled out*, *shoved away*, *fling out*.

The verbs clearly denote the nervousness and confusion in Dev's mind.

Grammatical Categories

Sentence length. The first sentence is the longest. It denotes the complexity of ideas in Dev's mind. The last is the shortest; it points to the emerging clarity of ideas a result of his thinking. The multiplicity of coordinate structures with two relative clauses in sentence (1) and (4) suggest the thronging impressions on the mind of emigrant Dev. From sentence (2-10), the unsettled state of Dev is pictured, while sentence (11), resolves the conflict : He who wants tea must get up and make it. Dev has to rise to the situation, meet the challenge and make his stay in England a success.

The brevity and force of the last sentence makes it very emphatic, after the description of the fluctuating state of mind in the middle sentences.

Adverb clauses of time, place, manner and condition emphasise cause-effect relationship.

Prepositions are quite a few in number in the passage. Although a great deal of syntactic complexity seems to be arising out of prepositional phrases, these phrases relieve the description from over-abstraction. They concretize perception and facilitate conception. The role of *OF* in particular is to relate ideas to physical objects and sounds. *e.g., the bright bead curtain* (*Imaginary*), *OF bird and bottle sounds.* (Real).

As the keels and hulls	(Imaginary),
OF sound old boats	(Real).
Momentary bitterness	(Thought process),
OF the cup of tea	(Physical).
The wash and swell	(Ideational),
OF another day	(Physical).

Punctuation

The specific use of colon (:) is noteworthy.

Adit Sen and his wife Sarah likely to do this for him : (Sent. 9). A long pause in this sentence is to confirm the silence in the other part of the house, it also implies reflection on the part of Dev.

Again in sent. (11), his first day in London taught *him* (:) he who wants tea must get up and make it. The function of colon in this sentence is to separate the aphorism from the main sentence.

Figures of Speech

The passage is full of symbolic words and structures explaining and intensifying the one day old emigrant situation.

(i) *Parallel Constructions.* It is easy to find pairs like the following :

> *had died — had weathered. excitement and buoyancy — tiredness and bitterness. reached through — scrubbled through.*

Metaphor and Simile

Most of the images occur in the first paragraph, where a

constant assessment of the foreign situation is going on in the mind of Dev. The objective correlatives of the subjective feelings increase reader involvement.

Metaphors

New leafed hedges — suggests trimmed hedges.

Bright bead curtain of bird and bottle sounds — suggests tinkling sounds produced by chirping of birds and milk bottles, as heard by Dev in his half asleep state.

Giggling-tease — suggests an act of friendliness (an example of personification also).

Milky-fingers, (personification as well as metaphor), suggests white, liquid light in the morning.

An eiderdown smothered silence — suggests soft, luxurious living, which impels people to live in detachment.

Simile

As the keels and hulls of sound old boats — suggests that survival is a test based on day to day routine, the success of which depends on the strength of one's being.

Synecdochi

Wash and swell — represents the rising falling tidal motion.

Elegant variation

The blue quilt and *the blue satin* both have been used for the quilt.

Antithesis

Began too late, ended too early.

Phonological schemes

Alliteration

The title itself is alliterative *Bye-Bye Black Bird.*

Bird and Bottle sounds. face the window now swimming with/ liquid light.

Assonance

Clinking, clanking, giggling. These words are intrinsically *onomatopoeic* also.

Cohesion

In this passage, the use of articles as co-reference links is interesting to note.

Generic Reference

The use of indefinite article (7) coupled with abstract ideas suggests familiarity and normalcy. *A groan a giggling tease*, *a night's sleep*, *a tranquilizing smoke*, *a mother*, *a servant*, *a newly made fire*, *a cup of tea* etc. The underlying comparison between the two life styles continues unconsciously, as revealed by these habitual modes of thinking.

Specific Reference

Occurs (21) times in the passage. Only thrice it has been used with abstract nouns (*the wash and swell*, *the tiredness and bitterness*, *the support*), otherwise, the definite article is used with concrete objects. This consistent use of definite article with physical objects emphasises the fact of their unchangeability and permanence, while Dev's behaviour has been introduced with indefinite noun phrases, to make him stand out as someone in unfamiliar surroundings.

Repetition is a common device of Anita Desai to ensure cohesion. Words are consistently repeated *e.g.*, the *window* is repeated (4) times, *pillow* (2), *leap* (3), *milk*, *milky* (2), *bird and bottle* (2), *steady* (2), *half-smothered*, *smothered* (2), times. Besides these, the use of personal pronouns and demonstratives is frequent.

Context

The passage is a masterly combination of verbal artistry and psychological insight. From the first word to the last, an underlying pattern with minute detail is manifest.

The morning light is shown progressing downward. It touches the *telephone wires*, *television aerials*, the *drain pipes*, the *milk bottles*, the *brass door knockers* and the *new-leafed hedges*. The writer exhibits an uncanny choice of words. All these objects are man made; the two objects of nature, *hedge* and *milk*, are also shown under man's control. The hedge is trimmed and the milk is bottled. The birds and bottles are described as *clinking* and *clanking*. While clinking apart from suggesting the sharp sound of glass, also suggests the prison or lock up, and clanking suggests the sound of chains. Man in a city is all locked up and chained.

The mention of *lane lengths* in the beginning is the narrow limited world of man these days. The *informal good morning voices* and *politely* suggest a welcome. The welcome is informal but not familiar. *Politeness* suggests courtesy, not closeness.

Dev, a stranger in the country, can feel the welcome, but due to lack of familiarity feels disgusted, pulls out *the watch* (the watch represents time, an inanimate object brought with him from India), thinks that it might have failed to acclimatize itself, but finds it ticking steadily. Hence it is not the material world which has changed but rather the mental.

Dev tries to evade time, shoves the watch away with a groan, but it is still very near him. Next he realises that the window was left open by *mistake*. This was the second mistake discovered since the day break. He feels the cold, the white morning light seems to be teasing him; cajoling him into acceptance of a different weather. His winter coverings (the cover of his Indian attitudes and experiences) fail to ward off the cold. He has to face the window, which seems to be swimming, but the figures and colour of roofs and walls of adjoining houses are as *steady* as the *keels and hulls of sound old boats*. The haziness lies in the vision of the onlooker, not in the objects, they have proved their stability. The reality and acceptance of time is established with the use of the word *steady*. *Steady* ticking of the watch, steady as the sound old boats. Time does not stop, it is for Dev to weather this new life in England. The use of *another day's tidal wave*, is again suggestive that the battle of life has to be fought from day to day.

Dev *props and supports* himself, which is something very essential for survival. He tries to remember the good times, but physical and mental fatigue keeps him from feeling refreshed. Although the morning light is there, he *gropes* for cigarettes retrieves them from the brass knobbed dresser at the far end of the room. *The far end*, suggests the limitations of a newcomer. He leaves his *dishevelled bed* — the writer could have some other epithet but prefers *dishevelled*, meaning lack of order, symbolising the confusion in the mind of Dev. Dev *leaps* into the air. The word *leap* has been used thrice, emphasising the nervousness felt by him. He finds the floor cold, freezing, snatching cigarettes and matches, he tries to regain warmth and the feeling of comfort. He tries to keep the ashes from falling on the quilt, which shows his sense of respect for the new environment.

He thinks of India, Indian customs, the morning prayer, the mother son relationship (even grown up sons are dependent on the mother), the *scorched* and *sooty* servant boy (the poverty of India), *the newly made fire* (the backwardness of India). Dev realizes that he cannot dream of dependence (in such matters as a cup of tea), on his host and his wife, Adit and Sarah. The *eiderdown-smothered silence*, hints at the luxurious living, impelling people to lead lives of detachment. The cigarette, a temporary tranquilizer, dwindles. He leaps up again to fling it out into the hedge. He once again *faces the window*, means faces reality and realizes that the only way to get relief is to make a cup of tea for himself. He wraps his earthen brown shawl (earth symbolises reality), and goes to the kitchen. He has learnt his first lesson, on his first day in London : He who wants tea, must get up and make it.

The contrast in life styles, and in the ways of thinking is also made explicit with the foregrounded use of *but*. *But* has been used in the beginning of two sentences and once in the middle. Dev fails to judge reality in the beginning, but in the end he has to accept it.

The symbolism revealed by the passage, as studied through the words and structures, leaves one spellbound. From particular to universal, to use the Aristotlean phrase, Dev has to accept the physical conditions of change, redefine human relations, and reform his attitude towards life : the basic requirements for a person in a foreign country.

WHERE SHALL WE GO THIS SUMMER[21] (Novel IV)

Text from *Where Shall We Go This Summer*?

Moses waited (1). Waiting was what he did most of his time : it was not only his prime but also his legitimate occupation (2) So, with some righteousness in the lift of his heavy chin, he left the shallow dinghy to loll on the muddy waves, leaving his own monumental patience behind on the narrow seat to guard the oars, and wrapping his brilliant lungi more closely, more attractively about his hips, went into the tea shop on the beach to which a transistor radio allured him by its trilling songs, so ripe with sensuous promise (3). He sat among jars of pink biscuits and cream horns and calendars with lush mythological themes and drank sweet tea out of a thick glass (4). He was served respectfully — it is not everyone who is paid, has been paid for twenty years, merely for waiting (5).

He was not altogether comfortable, however (6). It was growing steadily hotter and muggier under the low, hammered-out, tin can roof of the tea shop (7). The monsoon had temporarily withdrawn to the horizon, there to lie, visibly panting, collecting itself for another, stronger return, while on the land everyone waited — some with patience, some without — for the rain to begin again, and soon, with growing righteousness making his jaws ever heavier and stiffer and purpler (8). Moses rose and slipped through the back door of the shop into the smaller, darker, hotter precinct behind where only known and trusted customers such as Moses were permitted and welcomed (9). This was the domain of the tea owner's wife, Jamila (10). She cackled to see him come and served him his favourite cashew nut spirits in a thick, smeared glass and stood scratching her head with a long hairpin as she watched him drink (11).

At first, he drank alone (12). Later, as the afternoon dwindled hopelessly into evening, neighbours of his from the island and some mainland men he did not know who had come to trade at the open-air market in Marve, joined him and his drinking quickened in pace and became almost jovial (13). Waiting lay less heavily on him (14).

"Hey Moses," said Ali, "the caretaker of the neighbouring house on the island (15). All dressed up for the market, are you?" (16).

"Huh, the market," Moses belched in contempt (17). "Am I a trader ? (18). No, I am here on duty" (19). "Drinking duty, eh ?" (20). As they laughed, paying him back for his contempt, his eyeballs rolled like two porpoises making a brief appearance in the thick purple waves of his fleshy face (21). Then they sank soundlessly out of sight (22).

He remained silent, the others grew curious (23).

"Yes, that's a new lungi, isn't it?" remarked Joseph of the

diesel-oil pump (24). "And it isn't even time for the big fair in Bandra (25). That's when Moses usually goes gay" (26).

Moses gave the lungi a careless flick (27). It's checks of rose and maroon had about them the glow of square-cut gems — therefore it was not only a careless but also a proud flick (28). "I was sent twenty rupees," he admitted (29). "I had to spend it on something" (30).

"Twenty rupees! who would send you a big present like that — your mother-in-law" ? (31).

Analysis

A man called Moses, wearing a bright coloured lungi is waiting. We are told that he had been waiting for the past twenty years. He has come to this end of the shore in a dinghy, which he leaves unattended to enter a tea shop, where a trilling song is playing on a transistor radio. He is respectfully treated in the shop.

It is rainy season. People have been waiting for the monsoon which has temporarily retreated. Moses feels uncomfortable due to the stifling heat and enters the back room in the shop, where he is served cashewnut drinks by Jamila, the tea shop owner's wife.

Moses keeps drinking for hours on end, till he is joined by the men from the neighbourhood. The men tease Moses for his duty, which is merely *waiting*. They also tease him for the bright new lungi. Moses then gives out that he had bought it out of the twenty rupees sent to him.

General Observations

The passage is written in a mixed style. A combination of solid Saxon words with sophisticated, high sounding Latin words is present. One-third vocabulary consists of words of more than one syllable. Both formal and informal tones have been adopted. The writer makes free use of compound words, mostly to denote physical objects and places *e.g.*, ***hammered out***, ***tin-can roof***, *hairpin*, *main-land*, *diesel oil-pump*.

Nouns and Noun phrases. These mostly describe the village tea-shop atmosphere, interspersed with abstract nouns and adjectives, almost epical in nature *e.g.*, ***prime and legitimate occupation***, ***righteousness***, ***monumental***, ***mythological***, ***patience***, *precinct*, *domain*, *spirits*, *contempt*, *appearance*, *pace*. These words denote moral qualities and perceptions and have a regal air about them.

Proper Nouns include *Moses* (7), *Jamila*, *Joseph*, *Ali*, *Marve* (place), *Bandra* (place).

Collective Noun. *Market*.

Adjectives. The passage has a number of epithets which describe both psychological and physical states *e.g.*, *prime*, *legitimate*, *monumental*, *trilling*, *brilliant*, *sensuous*, *known*, *trusted*, *favourite*, *careless*, *proud*, *comfortable*, *brief*, all subjective in nature. The objective adjectives include, *heavy*, *muddy*, *narrow*, *sweet*, *thick*, *hotter*, *muggier*, *stronger*, *heavier*, *darker*, *smaller*, *long*, *new*, and colour adjectives *pink* and *purple* and *maroon*. As evident from the list, there is a noticeable number of adjectives of comparative degree. These are used with reference to the monsoon and the tea shop. The realm of Moses has been juxtaposed with the little world of Moses.

Adverbs. Three major classes of adverbs are included — manner, direction and time. The adverbs of manner predominate and emphasise the qualities of Moses.

Verbs are frequent in the passage. They refer to actions, events, physical acts, speech acts and psychological states. Almost an equal number of transitive and intransitive verbs balance the subjective and objective activities. The theme words *waited* and *waiting* have been used (5) times. The present participles include *waiting*, *growing*, *collecting*, *making*, *drinking*. These participles also happen to be the leading verbs in the passage.

Grammatical Categories

The passage has (9) simple and (22) complex sentences, out of which (5) are interrogative, the rest are declarative. Minor sentence types consist of two verbless sentences. The three long sentences are (2, 7 and 12). Complexity is mainly due to subordination, in which adverbial clauses predominate. There are three anticipatory structures adding suspense to the narration. Participial clauses and phrases (8), in number, add speed and compression to the narration. There is inversion in sentence (7 and

9). *e.g.*, *The monsoon had temporarily withdrawn to the horizon, there to lie.* (Sent. 7).

(The stress is on the word *there*, it is the place which is important.)

"*Am I a trader*?" (Sent. 19).

(A rhetorical sentence to express surprise and contempt, implying negation.)

Sentence (8) is an ambiguous construction, as both *It* and *He* have been used for the monsoon, which has been personified, and since the preceding and succeeding sentences are about Moses, the intention of the writer is not clear.

Schemes

The various figures of speech employed, support the underlying pattern of irony and open ridicule.

Hyperbole. The use of words like *monumental*, *prime*, *legitimate*, *precinct*, *domain*, all give exaggerated importance to Moses and his qualities.

Simile

His eye balls rolled like two porpoises (Sent. 21).

A conventional simile, which has a synaesthetic effect. The shifty nature of Moses exposed through his eyes, set in the dark, fleshy face is emphasised. Although far-fetched, they also carry further the analogy of monsoon clouds in the far distance, which now and then flash with lightning, which soon disappears. Moses himself was seen only sometimes, rest of the time he remained obscured to the world.

Quasi simile. *Cackled*. An example of *quasi simile*, suggesting the cheap talkative manner of Jamila. *Had the glow of square cut gems*. Another quasi-simile, implying comparison with gems. Moses has been portrayed having the manner of a lord, as such, the gems in his apparel are normal adornments.

Pathetic Fallacy

The monsoon has been described with human attributes.

'The monsoon had temporarily withdrawn to the horizon, there to lie, visibly panting, collecting itself for another stronger return;

while on land everyone waited — some with patience, some without — for the rain to begin again, and soon, with growing righteousness making his jaws ever heavier and stiffer and purpler' (Sent. 7).

The description of the monsoon has been juxtaposed with Moses. Moses lifts up his heavy chin with *some righteousness* (Sent. 3). The monsoon also with *growing righteousness* makes his jaws... (Sent. 8). Righteousness, a human attribute, used for the monsoon, makes the comparison prominent. The use of comparative constructions for the monsoon as well as the weather in the room at the small tea shop exposes the vanity and puny nature of Man (Moses), against the mighty powers of nature. Just as the monsoon disappears for long months and makes only seasonal appearance, in like manner, Moses also makes his appearance occasionally. After the long passivity of waiting, he has to gear himself by drinking. Like Moses, the monsoon clouds also have to fill themselves up for renewed activity.

Antithesis

Some with patience some without (Sent. 8).

Anaphoric Reference

It is not everyone *who is paid*, *has been paid* for twenty years, merely for waiting (Sent. 5).

Elegant variation : Spirits for drink

Irony

A close reading of the text reveals that words used do not just have face value, but are indicators of the underlying meaning and intention of the writer. A deliberate patterning for the purpose of irony and ridicule cannot escape careful reading.

The very first sentence, *Moses waited*, with an intransitive verb, creates suspense. In the second sentence, the definition of waiting has two very sophisticated words, *prime* and *legitimate*, which in the beginning seem out of place. The third sentence further intensifies the impression, *where loll* (a very commonplace word), is coupled with *monumental patience*. The personification of *patience*, an abstract quality, unseen, intangible, creates a suspicion of ridicule, which is confirmed when Moses enters the wayside tea shop consciously wrapping his *brilliant lungi*, *more closely*

(Sent. 5). Sentence (5) tells us that he was served respectfully, because he was paid for twenty years *merely* for waiting. The use of the focusing adjunct, *merely*, further confirms the sarcastic tone. Moses had been waiting, doing nothing. The conjunct, *however*, in sentence (6) points to the fact that, easy waiting was not altogether comfortable for him, because the tea shop, a shack, was becoming hotter and muggier. Anita Desai purposely uses compound words to describe the cheap material of which the shop's roof was made. A detailed description of the monsoon (Sent. 8), followed by the mention of the small room at the back of the tea shop; both described in comparative degrees of adjectives, foreground the analogy between Moses and the monsoon. The inclusion of the words *precinct*, *domain*, and *spirits*, to describe the cheap place, change the tone to open ridicule. Juxtaposed with the high sounding words above are *cackled*, *thick smeared glass*, *Jamila scratching her head with a hair pin* (Sent. 11).

(Lord), Moses drinks alone (Sent. 12). Previously it was stated that the domain of Jamila was only for the known and trusted, now Moses is joined by a group of people, known and unknown to him (Sent. 13). Moses becomes *jovial* (another word of mythological origin). His waiting lay less heavily on him (Sent. 13). Perhaps, because he had left his *monumental patience behind* in the dinghy! This is again a pun on *waiting*.

The conversation recorded between sentence (15) and (25) contains vulgar expressions like, *Hey*, *Huh*, *eh*, *belched*, etc. The men in the room ridicule Moses for his nature of duty. He is unable to answer back, and only rolls his eyes to show his anger (Sent. 21). The writer chooses Joseph of the diesel-oil pump, to provoke Moses to speak, or in other words inflame Moses to talk. The generic reference to a *careless flick* and *a proud flick*, again bestow on him the manner of a lord. His lungi also has the squares which glow like square cut gems. His megalomania is by now fully established.

This ingenious network of irony can be traced on a different plane also. In the first instance the word *waiting* was foregrounded, in the second, it is *righteousness*. The writer emphasises righteousness in Moses and righteousness in the monsoons. Some of the other indications of contrast, resulting in sarcasm are as follows :

(i) *Wrapping* his brilliant lungi *more closely more attractively* about *his hips* (Sent. 2).

(Moses likes to display his body beautiful!)

(ii) To which a transistor radio *allured* him by its *trilling songs* so *ripe* with *sensuous promise* (Sent. 3).

(Moses is allured by a life of flesh.)

(iii) He sat among jars of *pink* biscuits and *cream* horns and calendars with *lush* mythological themes and drank *sweet* tea (Sent. 4).

(The connotative use of *pink*, *lush*, and *sweet*.)

(iv) This was the domain of the tea shop — *owner's wife Jamila* (Sent. 10).

(Shows familiarity with the mistress and not the master!)

(v) The afternoon *dwindled hopelessly* (Sent. 13).

(The transferred epithet highlights the quality of Moses' waiting).

(vi) *Waiting lay less heavily* on him (Sent. 14).

(Contrasted with his monumental patience).

(vii) *Drinking duty* (Sent. 20).

(The enjoyable nature of his righteous duty!)

(viii) His eyeballs rolled like two porpoises making a brief appearance in the thick *purple* waves of his *fleshy* face (Sent. 21).

(*Purple* is the colour of royalty, *fleshy* has amusing connotations!)

(ix) When Moses *goes gay*.

(A happy abandon!)

All the above references clearly indicate the epicurean nature of Moses. Step by step the righteousness of Moses is blown to pieces. The message, man's hypocricy and insignificance compared with the mighty powers of nature, is made manifest with the help of clarifying statements and movement of images from an otherwise commonplace occurrence. Reader's reaction — A piece of art !

FIRE ON THE MOUNTAIN[22] (Novel V)

Text from *Fire on the Mountain*

Nanda Kaul paused under the pine trees to take in their scented sibilance and listen to the cicadas fiddling invisibly under the mesh of pine needles when she saw the postman slowly winding his way along the Upper Mall (1). She had not gone out to watch for him, did not want him to stop at Carignano, had no wish for letters (2). The sight of him, inexorably closing in with his swollen bag, rolled a fat ball of irritation into the cool cave of her day, blocking it stupidly : bags and letters, messages and demands, requests, promises and queries, she had wanted to be done with them all, at Carignano (3). She asked to be left to the pines and cicadas alone (4). She hoped he would not stop (5).

Everything she wanted was here, at Carignano, in Kasauli (6). Here, on the ridge of the mountain, in this quiet house (7). It was the place, and the time of life, that she had wanted and prepared for all her life — as she realized on her first day at Carignano, with great, cool flowering of relief — and at last she had it (8). She wanted no one and nothing else (9). Whatever else came, or happened here, would be an unwelcome intrusion and distraction (10).

This she tried to convey to the plodding postman with a cold and piercing stare from the height of the ridge onto his honest, bull back (11). Unfortunately he did not look up at her on the hill-top but stared stolidly down at the dust piling onto his shoes as he plodded on (12). A bullock man, an oafish ox, she thought bitterly, and averted her eyes (13). She stopped backwards into the garden and the wind suddenly billowed up and threw the pine branches about as though to curtain her (14). She was grey, tall and thin and her silk sari made a sweeping, shivering sound and she fancied, she could merge with pine trees and be mistaken for one (15). To be a tree, no more and no less, was all she was prepared to undertake (16).

What pleased and satisfied her so, here at Carignano, was its barrenness (17). This was the chief virtue of all Kasauli of course — its starkness (18). It had rocks, it had pines (19). It had light and air (20). In every direction there was a sweeping view — to the north, of the mountains, to the south, of the plains (21).

Occasionally an eagle swam through this unobstructed mass of light and air (22). That was all (23).

And Carignano, her home on the ridge, had no more than that (24). Why should it (25). The sun shone on its white walls (26). Its windows were open — the ones facing north opened on to the blue waves of the Himalayas flowing out and upto the line of ice and snow sketched upon the sky, while those that faced south looked down the plunging cliff to the plain stretching out; flat and sere, to the blurred horizon (27).

Analysis

Nanda Kaul, an old woman, lives all by herself in a remote house in Kasauli. The house is named Carignano. She does not wish to have any contact with the outside world. All she wants is to be one with the trees and cicadas surrounding her house.

The postman, who is the link between Carignano and outside world is detested by her. She scorns him for being an intruder and a beast of burden.

Nanda Kaul likes the barrenness and starkness of Kasauli and Carignano, especially Carignano, which promises her the much longed for relief after a life of duty and obligation. The house is full of light and air, with the snow-capped Himalayas on one side, and a plunging cliff on the other, leading on to a stretch of plain ground, with a blurred horizon.

General Observations

Our first impression of the passage is mixed. A woman lives alone in a secluded house. She is full of bitterness and repulsion towards the rest of the world. She finds Carignano a place of rest and refuge, bounded by the natural features as well as the hatred she feels towards the world in general. The setting of the house in Kasauli is ideal for her, with its starkness and barrenness, the rocks, the plentiful light and air.

Nouns. The foregrounded proper nouns and concrete nouns are *Nanda Kaul* (1), *Carignano* (6), *Kasauli* (2), *pine* (5), *Cicadas* (2), *Postman*, *bag*, *letters*, *wind*, *mountains*, *plain*, *eagle*, *light*, *air*, *the Himalayas*, *snow*, *cliff*.

A few abstract nouns are prominent too, *e.g.*, *sibilance*, *irritation*, *messages*, *demands*, *requests*, *promises*, *queries*, *intrusion*, *height*, *distraction*, *stare*, *life* (2), *relief*, *sound*, *barrenness*, *starkness*, *distraction* etc.

Adjectives are not very frequent in the passage. They refer to physical, visual and psychological states. There is an almost equal number of adjectives with positive and negative connotation, *e.g.*, *pine*, *scented*, *cool*, *great*, *honest*, *clear* etc. A few with neutral tones are, *white*, *blue*, *fat*, *bullock*, *unobtrusive*. Negative adjectives include *swollen*, *unwelcome*, *oafish*, *plodding*, *plunging*, *sore*, *blurred* and *shivering*.

Adverbs. The adverbs of direction, manner and degree are frequent in the passage. The adverbs of manner are all negative in connotation, *viz*., *invisibly*, *slowly*, *stupidly*, *inexorably*, *stolidly*, *unfortunately*, *bitterly*.

Verbs are almost all stative. They describe the mental state of Nanda Kaul. The passage has very little physical activity. Keen mental activity is foregrounded.

Words with Pejorative Meanings and Denoting Negation

The passage has an unusually large number of words and phrases with pejorative meaning and words denoting negation, *i.e.*, *sibilance*, *irritation*, *intrusion*, *distraction*, *stare*, *barrenness*, *starkness*, *to be done with them all*, *the sight of him*, *blocking*, *plodding*, *oafish*, *swollen*, *sere*, *blurred* etc.

These are all direct negative expressions.

Grammatical Categories

Sentence length is 18.1 words per sentence. Only three simple sentences are present the rest are all complex. The beginning and the end sentences are the longest. Sentence complexity is a reflection of thought complexity. Nanda Kaul, almost a misanthrop, is far from being normal. In the last sentence her adamant choice of living all by herself is reinforced.

Paragraph (2, 4 and 6), state Nanda Kaul's choices and the reasons for her preferences. These paragraphs have short sentences with frequent pauses. They correspond with the fragmented thinking of Nanda Kaul. They also summarize and interpret the motives of her choice. *That was all* (Sent. 23). *Why should it* ? (Sent. 25).

To support the brevity of sentences, a large number of monosyllabic words are included, which indicate the firmness and finality with which these choices are made. Two *rhetorical questions*, *What pleased and satisfied her so* (Sent. 17), and *Why should it*? (Sent. 25), entail a strong negative assertion, contradicting the very choices she has made. In the sentence, *This was the chief virtue of all Kasauli of course — its starkness* (Sent. 18), *this*, — a demonstrative pronoun used as a relative antecedent has an emotive reference. (Quirk and Greenbaum, p. 107).

Passive Constructions

To be done with them all (Sent. 3).

To be left to the pines (Sent. 5).

Was prepared to undertake (Sent. 16).

In the first sentence, Nanda Kaul wants to be alone in her self-imposed isolation. In the second, she importunes the world to leave her alone. The third reveals that she was willing to be a pine as a matter of responsibility and not repose, the phrase, was prepared, hints that her choice was something imposed on her by her circumstances or someone else.

Figures of Speech

The passage is based on the movement of images and hence from the first sentence to the last rhetorical devices can be traced.

Metaphors

The function of this figure of speech in this passage is to portray the internal conflict in the mind of Nanda Kaul, and symbolise it objectively through a situation. Therefore, metaphors in this passage are more illuminating than ornamental.

(i) *Swollen bag* (Sent. 3).

(ii) *Rolled a fat ball of irritation into the cool cave of her day* (Sent. 3).

These intensify the height of bitterness and scorn felt by Nanda Kaul. They also highlight the foolish choice : A cave is generally blocked from all sides except one, and so whatever little light and air pass through Nanda Kaul's self made habitat, that is blocked because of the violent reactions to the sight of other individuals.

(iii) *Cool flowering of relief* (Sent. 8).

This states the climax of bliss felt by her.

(iv) *Honest bull back, oafish ox, bullock man* (Sent. 11 and 12).

These reveal the contemptuous attitude of Nanda Kaul towards the people of lower status. She attributes the quality of simplicity and honesty to the postman, who is lost in himself. She disdainfully compares him not only with an animal, but an elfish deformed creature.

(v) *To be a tree* (Sent. 16).

This is another expressive image, which confirms Nanda Kaul's morbid choice. She knows she is not a tree, but wishes to be mistaken for one. The image reveals deliberate self-deception.

(vi) *Blue waves of the Himalayas, plunging cliff* (Sent. 27).

These two metaphors present hydro images, solid and collosal objects are viewed by Nanda Kaul as liquid, and associated with boundless and deep waters. A self-created exile.

(vii) *Snow sketched, line of ice* (Sent. 27).

For Nanda Kaul, boundaries and outlines are important, not the substance of things. A sketch gives the impression of an object, and a line of ice, marks the limits of vision.

Parallel Constructions

Pleased and satisfied (Sent. 17).

Barrenness and starkness (Sent. 17 and 18).

It had rocks, it had pines (Sent. 19).

Parallelism helps to enhance thematic prominence.

Antithesis

No more and no less (Sent. 16).

(i) *Scented sibilance* (Sent. 1).

The very first sentence contains this contradictory phrase. *Scented* has positive connotations, and *sibilance*, negative, representing a sound of disapproval and derision. Nanda Kaul a fine bred woman, well off in life, chooses a life of derision and scorn.

The theme thus stated in the beginning foretells the symbolic weight of the writing.

(ii) *No more and no less* (Sent. 16).

Denotes a sense of finality.

Zoological Images

Cicadas and eagle

Cicadas are small, insignificant, sheltered, creatures living in darkness, whereas eagle (indirectly Nanda Kaul herself), is big, regal, a bird of prey which soars in a sea of light and air. For Nanda Kaul cicadas are ever present and she wishes to listen to them constantly. She also likes to see the eagle soaring high, but it is seen only sometimes. Symbolically, it is not the grandeur but the meanness of life, of which she perpetually wishes to be reminded.

Tropes

Phonoaesthetic effects are clearly visible in frequent couplings in the passage.

Scented sibilance. /sentid sibilens/.

Cool cave. /ku:l keiv/.

Plodding postman. /plodiŋ poustmæn/.

Silk sari made a sweeping, shivering sound.

/silk sa:ri meid ə 'swi:piŋ ' ivriŋ 'saund/.

Barrenness, starkness/bærennes sta:knes/

Even phonetic analysis reveals contradictions. The word *unobstructed*, has five plosives /b/, /t/, /k/, /t/ and /d/. / obs'tr ktid, with a combination of central, back and front vowels, which makes it difficult to pronounce. It is quite opposite to the *free flow* for which it stands in the context.

Irony

Anita Desai suggests ambivalences of meaning by subtle

deviations from the expectations of the reader. The metaphors quoted above tend to serve the purpose of irony, which is the over arching figure in this passage.

The sarcasm implied is gradually introduced, till it becomes unavoidable in the last paragraph.

Nanda Kaul prefers the *scented sibilance* of pines, a contradictory choice. She thinks that the sight of the *swollen bag of the postman, blocks the cool cave of her day, with a fat ball of irritation* (Sent. 3). A cave after all is already an enclosed place with a single entrance. In the second paragraph, suspense is created by the description of the realisation of a dream. The specific requirements of Nanda Kaul are not mentioned. The third para opens with Nanda Kaul looking down at the postman, from the heights of Carignano. Sentence (12), begins with *unfortunately*, an attitudinal disjunct (Quirk and Greenbaum, p. 242). For whom was the stare unfortunate? Nanda Kaul wished the postman to look up and apprise himself with her indignation, but unfortunately he does not look up. Next, Nanda Kaul wishes to *be mistaken* for a tree (Sent. 16). It was something she was willing to undertake. To be one with nature is self-realization, but to consider it a responsibility is obliging nature itself!

In the fourth para, the virtues of Kasauli listed, hardly recommend the place. Overtly negative terms have been suggested as good qualities. *Barrenness* associated with fruitlessness and *starkness*, implying rigidity and stiffness, something devoid of cover and adornment have been considered the attractions of the place. The *rocks* and *tall pines*, further confirm the solid surroundings. The words *light and air* are repeated in the passage (Sent. 20 and 22), but the soil to generate new life is lacking. In this vast, empty mass of light and air, an eagle (Nanda Kaul), soars alone to prey on creatures (like the postman), inferior to it. The para ends with three mono-syllabic words, *That was all* (Sent. 23), emphasising the confined nature of possibilities the place afforded.

The passage reaches its point of concentration in the last para. The restricted appeal of the place is reiterated in, *had no more than that* (Sent. 24). A rhetorical question follows *why should* it? (Sent. 25). A positive rhetorical question strengthens strong negation. *Barrenness* and *starkness* are attributes to be evaded rather than prized. Nanda Kaul's unusual choices are now confirmed. Further, the *sun shone on its white walls* — white walls here suggest blankness. Its windows were open (Sent. 26), not the doors. Generally, the prison windows are kept open too. And what view do these windows afford? The sea of the Himalayas on one side (the blue waves of the Himalayas (Sent. 27), and the flat sere plain with a blurred horizon on the other — both suggest the reign of uncertainty and insecurity.

Nanda Kaul was deceived in believing that she had found a place of refuge. She thought that she would be a pine, towering above the cicadas *i.e.*, the rest of the world, living in the mesh of its needles, symbolising her old rejected world. But the irony of it was that, even if she became a pine the cicadas will be there right near her roots.

The interlocking images thus complete the jigsaw puzzle of the passage. Each word and phrase is essential to complete the pattern intended by the author.

CLEAR LIGHT OF DAY[23] (Novel VI)

Text from *Clear Light of Day*

The koels began to call before daylight (1). Their voices rang out from the dark trees like an arrangement of bells, calling and echoing each other's calls mocking and enticing each other into ever higher and shriller calls (2). More and more joined in as the sun rose and when Tara could no longer bear the querulous demand in their voices, she got up and went out onto the verandah to find the blank white glare of the summer sun thrusting in between the round pillars and the purple bougainvillaea (3). Wincing, she shielded her eyes as she searched for the birds that had clamoured for her appearance, but saw nothing (4). The cane chairs on the verandah stood empty (5). A silent line of ants filed past her feet and down the steps into the garden (6). Then she saw her sister's figure in white, slowly meandering along what as children they had called 'the rose walk' (7).

Dropping her hands to pick up the hem of her long nightdress. Tara ran down the steps, bowing her head to the morning sun that came slicing down like a blade of steel onto the back of her neck, and crossed the dry crackling grass of the lawn to join her sister who stood watching, smiling (8).

The rose walk was a strip of grass, still streaked green and grey, between two long beds of roses at the far end of the lawn where a line of trees fringed the garden — fig and silver oak, mulberry and eucalyptus (9). Here there was still shade and, it seemed to Tara, the only bit of cultivation left; everything else, even the papaya and lemon trees, the bushes of hibiscus and oleander, the beds of canna lilies, seemed abandoned to dust and neglect, to struggle as they could against the heat and sun of summer (10).

But the rose walk had been maintained almost as it was (11). Or was it (12). It seemed to Tara that there had been far more roses in it when she was a child — luscious shaggy pink ones, small crisp white ones tinged with green, silky yellow ones that smelt of tea — and not just these small negligible crimson heads that lolled weakly on their thin stems (13). Tara had grown to know them on those mornings when she had trailed up and down after her mother who was expecting her youngest child and had been advised by her doctor to take some exercise (14). Her mother had not liked exercise, perhaps not the new baby either, and had paced up and down with her arms folded and her head sunk in thought while the koels mocked and screamed and dive-bombed the trees (15). Tara had danced and skipped after her, chattering, till she spied something flashing from under a pile of fallen rose petals — a pearl, or a silver ring? — and swooped upon it with a cry that broke into her mother's reverie and made her stop and frown (16). Tara had excitedly swept aside the petals and uncovered — a small, blanched snail (17). Her face wrinkling with disgust, her mother turned and paced on without a word, leaving Tara on her knees to contemplate the quality of disillusion (18).

Analysis

Tara wakes up with the call of Koels. She is on a visit to her childhood home. She walks through the garden and finds it dusty and neglected. She spots her sister on the rose walk, the part of the garden where once there used to be beautiful varieties of roses. She remembers the morning walks with her mother, who was expecting her last child, and was none the happy about it. The mother was often oblivious of the presence of Tara, and the small discoveries that the child made in the world of nature, did not excite her, but for Tara they were part of growing up.

General Observations

The language of the passage is simple with only 150 words of more than one syllable. The mode and style of discourse are formal and descriptive. Many words, specific to the register of horticulture are included. Particular use of parenthesis, mainly employed for elaboration, lends the passage an air of rumination.

Lexical Categories

Nouns. The number of concrete nouns (67), far exceeds that of abstract nouns (15). The abstract nouns describe perceptions and mental states. *e.g.*, *arrangement*, *voices* (2), *calls*, *calling* (3), *demand*, *disappearance*, *neglect*, *reverie*, *disgust*, *disillusion*, *frown*. It is noticeable that the words depicting mental states have all negative connotations. The *line of trees* (Sent. 9), suggests the boundary or limits of the garden.

Prominent Lexical Sets

(i) *Garden*, *trees*, *bougainvillaea*, *papaya*, *lemon*, *hibiscus*, *mulberry*, *eucalyptus*, different kinds of *roses*, *canna*, *lawn*, *rose walk*, *line of trees*, *grass*, *cultivation*, *bushes*, *silver oak*, *oleander*, etc.

(ii) *Koels*, *call*, *calls* (2), *calling*, *echoing*, *mocking*, *enticing*, *mocked*, *screamed*, *divebombed*, *voices*, *birds*, *line of ants*, *trailed*, *danced*, *skipped*, *swooped*, *snail* etc.

Common nouns for persons

sister, mother, child, children, doctor, new baby.

Proper noun. Tara (7).

Adjectives and adjectival phrases

These mostly refer to the physical states, *viz.*, *round*, small (2), *cane-chairs*, *dry crackling grass* etc. A large number of adjectives and participles create sensory images.

Audio — higher, *shriller*, *querulous*, *calling*, *echoing*, *mocking*, *enticing, screamed, chattering, visual — dark, blank, purple, pink, white, yellow, blanched, flashing.*

* *Tactile — shaggy, silky, crisp.*

* *Olfactory — smelt of tea.*

* *Gustatory — luscious, smelt of tea, crisp.*

Adverbs and Adverbial phrases

In all (21), in number out of which adverbs of manner are only (3), *weakly, slowly, excitedly*. Adverbs of direction and place are (11), of time (6) and adverbs denoting option only (1), *i.e., perhaps*.

Verbs. The passage is full of kinetic verbs, viz; *began to call, rang out, joined, shielded, searched, clamoured, filed past, crossed, swooped, uncovered, divebombed*, besides these the present participles quoted above also create kinetic images. Incidentally, these transitive verbs are associated with either abstract nouns, or denote unseen actions and objects or emptiness.

Examples :

(i) Their voices *rang out* from the dark trees like an *arrangement of bells* (Sent. 2).
(*Arrangement* — an abstract noun).

(ii) *calling and echoing each other's calls* (Sent. 2).
(*calls*, an abstract noun).

(iii) As she *searched* for the birds that *had clamoured* for her *appearance*, she saw *nothing* (Sent. 4).

(iv) The verandah chairs *stood empty* (Sent. 5).

(v) Tara *stepped* on to the verandah *to find the blank white glare* (Sent. 3).

The intransitive verbs describe both physical states and mental processes *e.g., streaked green and grey* (Sent. 3), *A line of trees fringed the garden* (Sent. 9), *seemed to Tara, seemed abandoned to dust and neglect* (Sent. 10), *maintained almost as it was* (Sent. 11).

Another prominent feature of the passage is the use of present participles. In all (18) in number, they add speed and compactness to the writing. They are mostly used in the first paragraph, where maximum activity in the present takes place. Para (3 and 4), are given to comparison with the past, and since the process of recollection is a slow one, present participles have been discreetly left out. Towards the end of the fourth paragraph, we have four of them in a row — *chattering*, *flashing*, *wrinkling*, *leaving*. Here they restrain Tara's reminiscences, and further, the progression of the story.

Tenses. The first three paragraphs are written in simple past, whereas the last paragraph has past perfect tense. This effectively denotes the gap in years. The reader is taken back to Tara's childhood, the distance in years is made explicit.

Grammatical Categories

Total number of sentences in the passage is (18), with approximately (29) words per sentence. Except (2) interrogative sentences, all the remaining are declarative in nature. The two rhetorical questions, *Or was it*? (Sent. 12), and, *a pearl or a silver ring* (Sent. 16), add an element of unsurety, which is natural in the process of recollection.

The ratio of independent clauses to dependent clauses is 1:3. Complexity is due to all three — subordination, coordination and parataxis. Adverbials and premodification by adjectives also increase syntactic complexity. There are a number of verbless clauses, mainly included for the purpose of elaboration. They describe varieties of trees, plants and flowers. Sudden brevity of the sentence *Or was it*? summarizes and interprets the setting which the reader had so far watched only as an onlooker. It promotes human involvement in the narration.

Inversion

Here there was still shade (Sent. 10). The sentence highlights the contrast between the past and the present.

Scheme and Tropes

Metaphor and Simile

The passage has two conventional similes :

(i) Like an arrangement of bells (Sent. 1).

(ii) Like a blade of steel (used for sun rays, Sent. 8).

The writer uses expressions like, *as it was* (Sent. 11), seemed to, seemed (Sent. 10), which express similarity between the past and the present. Whether an illusion or reality, these sentences suggest ambivalences of meaning, a natural consequence of comparison of experience separated by years.

Analogy. There is an underlying analogy between the perceptions of a child and an adult. Tara tries to compare the *call of birds* in the distant past and the present. Tara's *reaction to light*, as a child and as an adult is also interesting to note. As a child, light brought disillusion to Tara (Sent. 18), as an adult, light is hurting to her (Sent. 4).

As an adult, Tara sees arrangement and organisation in nature, *i.e.*, an arrangement of bells (Sent. 1). She also defines the voices of the birds. The words *call* and *calling* occur three times in a single sentence. The relation between the birds is stressed (use of the phrase *each other*, in the same sentence). As a child the Koels were only mischievous birds to Tara, *dive-bombing*, *screaming*, *mocking*. The common words are *mocked*, *mocking*. The harmony which changes *mock* into *praise* or approval is lacking in both instances.

Phonological Schemes

A number of couplings mark the passage. *calling-echoing*, *higher-shriller*, *mocking-enticing*, *paced up and down-trailed up and down*. A whole range of present participles facilitate easy flow of sentences and allow the reader to concentrate more on the noun phrases and intransitive verbs describing mental processes.

Alliteration and *Assonance*.

Calling, enticing, echoing each other's calls, mocking and enticing each other into higher and shriller calls.

Cohesion and Context

The passage notably features not only lexical repetition, but contextual repetition as well. Tara wakes up with the call of Koels, and is reminded of the same voices as a child. She walks through the garden, and remembers the delightful roses of the rose walk in her childhood days. Morning sun was hurtful to her now, and even as a child, one of her encounters with reality took place in the morning light when she found a snail, instead of a pearl or a silver ring. This entails repetition of words plus associated experiences. Some common links are *koels*, *mocked*, *mocking*, *the rose walk*, and the *morning light*. The use of personal pronouns and definite article also contribute as co-reference devices.

Some interesting observations are associated with the use of the indefinite article (9), which Anita Desai uses sparingly. *A silent line of ants*, *a blade of steel*, *a line of trees*, *a child*, *a pile of fallen rose petals*, *a pearl*, *a silver ring*, *a cry*, *a small snail*, all these generic references express the attitude of Tara, (as the passage portrays her consciousness), and indicate the writer's intention. *A silent line of ants*, happens to be in the first paragraph, where the writer interprets Tara's thoughts for us. A generic reference for the disciplined ants points to Tara's casual attitude towards them. *A line of trees*, is referred to in the third paragraph, where the reader shares the consciousness of Tara, who finds certain things still there. The repeated use of *still* in the same sentence, coupled with the indefinite article, confirms that Tara takes the trees for granted, nothing special. *A blade of steel*, refers to the sharpness of pain, pain is more important than the cause of it. Likewise, generic references, *a child*, *a silver ring*, *a pearl*, *a cry*, make the distance in years and the insignificance of objects for Tara, more obvious.

On the whole the passage signifies a lack of harmony between nature and human beings. The call of Koels is interpreted as an arrangement of bells, something organised and yet Tara is unable to bear the *querulous demand*, *the clamouring*. The morning sun is painful, slicing like a blade of steel, Tara *winces* when she faces the morning light, which is a *blank glare* for her (Sent. 3). The line of ants goes unnoticed by. The garden is abandoned to *dust and neglect* (Sent. 10). The roses are thin weaklings, the mother does not want the new baby (Sent. 15). As a child Tara is disgusted to see the snail. She is more interested in pearls and silver than a tiny creature (Sent. 16). The human beings described in the passage, seem to be lost in their own worlds, rather than have any sympathy or understanding of the world around them. The clear light of day is scathing to an adult and brings disillusion to the child. But happiness lies in reconciling with it, recognizing its indispensible share in the process of creation and the sustenance of life.

A VILLAGE BY THE SEA[24] (Novel VII)

Text from *A Village by the Sea*

When Lila went out on the beach it was so early in the morning that there was no one else there (1). The sand was washed clean by last night's tide and no one had walked on it except the birds that fished along the coast — gulls, curlews and sandpipes (2). She walked down to the sea with the small basket she carried on the flat of her hand, filled with flowers she had plucked from the garden around their house — scarlet hibiscus blooms, sweet-smelling spider lilies and bright butter-yellow allamanda flowers (3).

When she came to the edge of the sea, she lifted the folds of her sari and tucked them up at her waist, then waded out into the waves that came rushing up over her feet and swirling about her ankles in creamy foam (4). She waded in till she came to a cluster of three rocks (5). One of them was daubed with red and white powder (6). It was the sacred rock, a kind of temple in the sea (7). At high tide it would be inundated but now, at low tide, it could be freshly consecrated (8). Lila took the flowers from her basket and scattered them about the rock, then folded her hands and bowed (9).

Just then the sun lifted up over the coconut palms in a line along the beach and sent long slanting rays over the silvery sand to touch her on the back of her head (10). Enjoying their warmth, she stayed bowed for a little while, her feet still in the cold, whispering wave (11). The sun lit up the pink and mauve waves with sparkles (12). Far out, stretched along the horizon, was the fishing fleet that had been out all night, the sails like white wings, or fins, lifting out of the sea (13). They were anchored and still they would not return before sundown (14). Later in the morning more women would come and offer flowers at the sacred rock (15). Some would say a little prayer for the safety of the fishermen at sea because they were all the wives and daughters of fishermen (16). Some would simply bow, like Lila, and say a greeting to God (17). It seemed a good way to start the morning (18). There was no real reason why they prayed in the rock rather than any other rock, but they needed something to which they could offer flowers and red kum-kum powder as they said their prayers, and the large flat-topped one that stood in the shallow water and was easy to approach was the most convenient one (19). It was not so far away as the temple in the village at the far end of the beach, nor did they need to give money to a priest who would perform the puja for them (20). The women preferred to do it themselves (21).

When Lila's father still owned a boat and went to sea to fish, her mother used to bring flowers to this rock in the sea, and pray.

Analysis

No one except birds had trod the beach when Lila, with a basket of flowers, reached there, to worship at the sacred rock in shallow waters. The sacred rock could only be worshipped during low tide. At high tide, it remained inundated. Lila, like the others had come to consecrate it with red and white powder and fresh flowers.

Lila performed the puja and bowed in worship. The morning sun was pleasing to her. There was an atmosphere of calm and peace. Everything seemed still, even the fishing fleet in the distance was still. The particular rock in front of which Lila stood, was chosen by the women of the village for its convenience. It was customary for them to pray in the morning, and the particular rock happened to be the easiest to approach. Instead of paying money to the priest for the task, the women preferred to worship by themselves in this safe spot. Lila's mother also used to offer flowers and pray near it, when Lila's father had a boat and a good business.

Our first impression of the passage is that of a slow moving film, showing us the morning beach with the sand washed clean by the night tide, and with claw marks of different birds. A girl carrying a small basket on the palm of her hand, filled with bright coloured flowers. On reaching the edge of the sea, she carefully tucks her sari, Wades into water, reaches the particular rock and performs her puja.

In the background is the rising sun, scattering its colourful rays on the scene. The girl seems to be enjoying the warm sun rays on her back and the cold waves on her feet. The scene has fishing boats along the horizon, anchored and still. There seems to be a commentary along with this slow motion picture. We are told why this particular rock has been given all the importance by the local women. In the end, it seems that the rock has been sacred for generations, as Lila's mother always used to offer kum-kum and flowers to the very same rock.

Lexical Features

Nouns. Being a physical description, the passage has a large number of concrete nouns, mostly relating to topographical details near the sea, *i.e.*, *sea*, *sand*, *coast*, *waves*, *rocks*, *palms* etc. Along with these the words associated with worship also tend to occur. *Flowers*, *kum-kum*, *puja*, *sacred*, *rock*, *temple*, *priest*, *prayers* etc.

Abstract Nouns are few but vital to the meaning *e.g.*, *God*, *good*, *real*, *reason*, all refer to the underlying values on which the description is based. Although the concrete nouns are repeated many times, it is the human element which has been given prominence.

Proper nouns. *Lila* and thereafter the *personal pronouns*, dominate the main noun phrases. The other common nouns relating to human beings and human relations are *women*, *priest*, *mother* and *father*.

The other nouns strikingly used are pertaining *to birds*, *flowers*, *the sun*, *the fishing fleet*, but all these form a background to the action of the lone character Lila. Abstract nouns, *edge*, *line*, *safety*, *horizon*, all refer to the physical limits and hence suggest a boundary, not only to the word picture drawn, but also to the world of Lila and the small village community.

Adjectives and Adverbs too add colour, quality and direction to the description. Anita Desai is famous for her sensuousness. In this passage also, we have *scarlet*, *yellow*, *red*, *white*, *silver*, *pink*, *mauve*, almost the whole spectrum. The largest group of adverbs is that of direction (25). These are combined with verbs which emphasise movement and activity. Other adverbs refer to time, thus lend pointedness to contextual meaning.

Compared to nouns (89), the main verbs (41) are lesser in number. Most verbs are dynamic (23), and indicate movements.

Even stative verbs have implications of physical activity *viz.*, *stood*, *prayed*, *approach*, *anchored*. Gradual amplification of an action is denoted by the repetition of verbs such as, *waded* (2), *walked* (2), *bowed* (2). The interesting point to note about verbs is that in the first three paragraphs, individual action of Lila is juxtaposed with the communal action of the women of the locality in the fourth paragraph. Here, simple past tense is changed to modal auxiliary *would* (Quirk and Greenbaum, p. 56), suggesting habitual action, *e.g.*, *would come*, *would bow*, *would say*, *would perform* etc.

In other words, the individual stands out against the background of society, of animate and inanimate objects. This observation is further strengthened by the fact, that even the nouns denoting inanimate objects are plural in number. This consistent use of plurality adds further prominence to the single figure of Lila.

Grammatical Features

Sentence length. Short sentences (12), predominate. There are only (3) long sentences of more than (40) words. These serve the purpose of post modification, detailed description of a physical act and explanation of an abstract idea. Only (4) sentences are simple. The rest are all complex. Six sentences have anticipatory structures, which provide a point of orientation and bring an element of suspense in the description. In fact, the passage begins with one. Each sentence is elaborated by coordination and subordination. By progressive elaboration, the reader is able to follow each movement in the temporal setting. The use of adverbial and relative clauses lends detail and vividness to the description.

Prepositions. Skilful use of prepositions, mainly for the purpose of direction, marks the passage, as in the sentence — *she waded out into the waves that came rushing up over her feet* (Sent. 4). In the first instance, the reference is to the vast expanse of water, in the second, the distance covered to reach the rock.

Punctuation. A special use of parenthesis, mainly for the purpose of post modification is made. *e.g.*, Birds that fished along the coast — gulls, curlews, and sandpipers (Sent. 2).

"Plucked from the garden around the house — scarlet hibiscus blooms, sweet smelling spider lilies, and bright butter-yellow alamanda flowers (Sent. 3)."

Figures of Speech

Simile and Metaphor

In this passage there is only one conventional simile — *sails like white wings and fins* (Sent. 13), all three words, sails, wings and fins denote locomotion. Comparison with wings and fins also juxtaposes the smallness of boats with the boundless waters of the sea.

Another simile in an unconventional manner is, *not so far away as the temple* (Sent. 19). The sacred rock is a kind of temple. An inherent comparison of distances, gives a natural tone to the description.

The two metaphors, *creamy foam* and *silvery sand*, create synaesthetic images, white *whispering waves*, has an animising effect and suggests hidden voices of the sea, the perennial mystery of elemental forces.

Phonological Schemes

The passage communicates its visual experience not only with intense realisation, but with a sense of beauty. This comes in part from patterns which have a phonoaesthetic effect, particularly pairing of like sounding words and phrases, as, waded out into, waded in (Sent. 4), walked on, walked *down* (Sent. 2, 3), hightide, lowtide (Sent. 8).

Examples of alliteration and assonance are easy to find :

(i) Sweet smelling spider lilies.

(ii) Bright butter-yellow alamanda flowers.

(iii) Fishing fleet.

(iv) White wings.

(v) Long slanting rays.

All long vowels, reinforce the visual effect.

Cohesion and Context

The passage is entirely a third person narration. There is no direct speech. The most notable feature of cohesion in the passage is lexical repetition of various kinds. Anita Desai repeatedly mentions the objects in the background, such as, the sea (5), rock, rocks (5), flowers (6), beach (3). Consistent use of simple past tense in the first three paragraphs and the use of *would* to denote habitual action in the past, in the fourth paragraph, also strengthen the impression of continuity. Personal pronouns (14), and the definite article (24), have also been used for cross-reference. The definite article promotes clarity, as it is mostly accompanied by a noun identifying a previous reference. Thus *the flowers* in (Sent. 9), refer back to *the flowers* introduced in (Sent. 2), the rock in (Sent. 7, 9, 15 and 19), all refer back to the rock in sentence (5).

Surprisingly, the indefinite article has been used only (7) times, in the whole passage, out of which (5) times the use is idiomatic. *A cluster of three rocks*, *a kind of temple*, coconut palms *in a line*, a *little prayer*, *a good way*, *a greeting to God*, *a priest*, *a boat*. This use of the indefinite article suggests the insignificance of formal arrangements for the village folk. Any rock can be worshipped, a temple is not a must for worship, a line of trees may be there just by chance, the length of prayer is not important, to worship in the morning is a good way, but not the only way, God is a well-known entity and hence a greeting is very normal on meeting, a priest is not a must for any worship, a boat is a medium of earning bread, but not the bread itself. For the simple village community, the faith, the underlying idea of worship and objects in themselves are more important than their appearance.

Other Contextual Features

Anita Desai uses three Hindi words : *puja*, *sari* and *kum-kum*, in this passage. The atmosphere of the story is peculiarly Indian. The daubing of the rock with red and white powder, the flora and fauna, the beliefs and customs of the fishing community, all combined, present a picture of an Indian village, situated on the sea shore depending on the 'Rock of Ages', for all that is precious in life.

***IN CUSTODY*[25] (Novel VIII)**

Text from *In Custody*

His first feeling on turning around at the tap on his shoulder while he was buying cigarettes at the college canteen and seeing his old friend Murad was one of joy so that he gasped 'Murad?

You?' and the cigarettes fell from his hand in amazement, but this rapidly turned to anxiety when Murad gave a laugh, showing the betel-stained teeth beneath the small bristling moustache he still wore on his upper lip (1 + 2). 'But I have a class just now, Murad,' he stammered as Murad squeezed his shoulders tightly as if he did not intend to let go (3).

'Stop worrying about your class,' Murad said, drawing him close to him and laughing into his ear (4). 'I've come all the way from Delhi to see you — can't you give me half an hour of your time?' (5).

'But it's Monday — not on Monday, Murad' (6).

'Oh, so friendship is only for Sunday, is it? Is that friendship?' Murad boomed (8).

They walked away from the canteen, across the dusty field that separated the corrugated iron shack of the canteen from the brick building of the college where Deven taught (9). Deven was aware that many of his students had observed this encounter with his old friend and were staring openly, some even smirking at the sight (10). He tried to wriggle out of Murad's grasp unobtrusively so as not to offend him (11).

'Just one more class, Murad,' he pleaded, 'then I'm free to go home' (12).

'Home? (13) Who wants to go home?' shouted Murad (14). 'We're going out to lunch (15). We're going to lunch in the best restaurant in your great city (16). If I come all the way from Delhi to see you, then you can at least give me a good lunch,' he added in a petulant voice (17).

'Of course, of course,' Deven assured him, feeling guilty at his lapse in hospitality (18). 'Here, have a cigarette, I bought two' (19). He fumbled in his shirt pocket for them and handed one to his friend (20).

'Still a two-cigarette man, are you?' Murad laughed holding one between his fingers and waiting for Deven to strike a match (21). As there was a March wind tearing across the open field and whirling dust and dry leaves around violently, this was a lengthy, fumbled business (22). When it was done at last and they strolled on, Murad said insolently, 'A full-fledged lecturer in a college, an important citizen of Mirpore, and still can't afford a whole packet of cigarettes? (23). You, seem to be where you were in your college days (24). What's the matter?' (25).

'No, no,' Deven hastened to explain (26). My wife has told me not to buy a packet at a time (27). She says if I have to go out to buy just one at a time, I will make smoke less' (28). He tried to laugh, as at a pleasant joke (29). 'Women are always trying to make you smoke less, drink less (30). You know' (31).

'Oh, so you do still drink, do you? (32). I'm glad to hear that,' Murad gave a yelp and another clap on Deven's shoulder (33). 'Will I get a drink with my lunch?' (34).

Analysis

The meeting of Deven with his old friend Murad, after a long time, in the college campus, where Deven is working as a lecturer, is the subject of this opening passage.

Murad has come all the way from Delhi to meet Deven, but Deven although happy to see him wants first to engage his class. Murad insists that he give up the class and join him for lunch in the best restaurant of the town. Deven offers him a cigarette and Murad takes this opportunity to taunt him about his straitened circumstances. Deven sheepishly tries to assure him that he is not so badly off. Murad bullies him further, and suggests that Deven offer him a drink to prove that.

General Observations

The passage is written in simple English, except a few Latin and French origin words *viz., encounter, unobtrusive, hospitality, restaurant* (French), *petulant*. A few compound words occur in the passage, sounding more Indian and cliche ridden, than original *e.g., a two cigarette man* — almost a translation of *do take ka admi, betel stained,* and *full-fledged,* are all stale idioms.

The language is conversational, exhibiting the typical features of Indian middle class speech.

Nouns and Noun Phrases. Out of (100) nouns included only (14) are abstract. *Feeling, anxiety, time, friendship* (2), *lapse, yelp, clasp, grasp, business, citizen, hospitality, matter, joke.* These words mostly depict emotional states and social qualities. There are a few lexical sets which are prominent.

Words associated with food and food places. Canteen (3), *Cigarettes* (3), *lunch* (4), *restaurant, drink, cigarettes* (2), *smoke.*

Words associated with College. College (2), *class* (3), *lecturer, studies.*

Words associated with time reference : Hour, time, Monday, Sunday, March, days.

The theme words can be called *Friendship* (2), *Friend* (4) and *hospitality.*

Proper nouns. Deven (5), *Murad* (9), *Delhi* (2), *Mirpore* (1).

Adjectives and Adjectival phrases. They are few in number. Some of them express physical states, like, *beetle-stained, two cigarette man, bristling, upper, dusty, corrugated, brick.* The others are evaluative in nature, as *old* (2), *best, good, fumbled, full-fledged, whole, college.* A single adjective with emotional connotation is '*petulant*'. Adjectives modify objective and subjective states alike.

Adverbs. There is a predominance of adverbs of manner — *rapidly, tightly, openly, unobstrusively, violently, insolently.*

Verbs. carry a very important part in the passage. In fact, they are key to the magic of the passage. Majority of the verbs are stative, concerned with speech acts and psychological states. Verbs used for Deven and Murad separately make an interesting study. The difference between the two characters is very obvious when we have a close look at the verbs. Some of the main verbs used for Deven and Murad separately are :

Deven	*Murad*
grasped	see
smirking	come
tried to wriggle	give
stammered	laughing
observed	going to
assured	going out
fumbled	laughed
strike	holding
hastened	walking
will make	will get
to make	to hear

The hesitation, lack of confidence, awkwardness in the behaviour of Deven, and the sense of finality and confidence in the behaviour of Murad are easily discernible.

Grammatical Categories

Being conversational in nature, the passage has declarative as well as other sentence types. There is one *imperative sentence.*

'*Stop worrying about your class*' (Sent. 4).

There are two *rhetorical sentences.*

Is that friendship, Is it? (Sent. 8).

Home? who wants to go home.

Weak forms are also used, *wasn't, we're.*

Cohesion and Context

The passage highlights the characters of Deven and Murad. The above linguistic features present two different personalities altogether.

Deven's (5) first feeling on seeing his old friend Murad was one of joy (Sent. 1). This feeling is soon turned into anxiety (Sent. 2). Deven is a nervous, self-conscious person. When Murad talks in loud tones, he is conscious of the students staring at him, even smirking at the sight (Sent. 10). The expressions used for Deven all confirm the above mentioned qualities in him.

He tried to *wriggle out* of Murad's grasp *unobtrusively* so as not to offend him (Sent. 11).

He *pleaded* before Murad to allow him to take his class when Murad wishes to have lunch in the best restaurant of the town, he sheepishly agrees, saying of course, of course (Sent. 17). He fumbled in his shirt pocket for his cigarettes. Again, while lighting the cigarette for Murad the writer comments, *'It was a fumbled business'* suggesting that there was awkwardness in the action. When Murad taunts him for his poor financial condition, instead of retaliating, he gently tries to explain. He is controlled by his wife also. Tries to pass it on as a pleasant joke.

'*My wife has told me not to buy a packet at a time. She says if I have to go out to buy just one at a time, I will make smoke less. He tried to laugh, as at a pleasant joke*' (Sent. 27-30). *Women are always trying to make you smoke less, drinkless* : *You know* (Sent. 32). Additional comments like this stress the importance of the listener, meaning, your understanding my point of view is important to me.

Deven emerges as a weak-willed man, nervous and lacking in self-confidence, but at the same time gentle caring and self-respecting. He feels sorry at his lapse in hospitality (Sent. 17). He wants to share with Murad whatever he has and wants to help him.

On the other hand we have Murad (9) who dominates the scene. The words associated with him and used by him all give an impression of an assertive, self-confident man, even to some extent unpolished and selfish, lacking in a sense of propriety.

The following examples support the view :

(i) *Murad gave a laugh, showing the betel stained teeth beneath the bristling moustache.* (Sent. 2)

(Eating betel leaf, although common, is not considered very respectable. Murad is not conscious of it, but Deven is.)

(ii) *Murad squeezed Deven's shoulders tightly as if he did not intend to let go.* (Sent. 3)

(Exhibition of familiarity in a public place is not very decent according to Indian standards).

(iii) *Stop worrying about your class.* (Sent. 4)

(An imperative sentence, Murad wants to assert control over Deven, at the same time, has little compunction for neglect of duty.)

(iv) *Drawing him close to him and laughing into his ear.* (Sent. 4).

(Lack of good manners.)

(v) *I've come all the way from Delhi to see you — Can't you give me half an hour of your time? 'Oh,' so friendship is only for Sunday, is it? Is that friendship? Murad boomed.* (Sent. 8)

(Rhetorical question — emotional exploitation of Deven.

Raises his voice, makes Deven self-conscious and hence more yielding.)

(vi) *Home*? *Who wants to go home*? *....petulant voice.* (Sent. 16)

(Shows disregard for Deven's home. Not much respect for familial ties. Intensifies emotional exploitation; by shouting and rejecting the idea. Bullies Deven to take him to the best restaurant. Adopts a querulous tone to completely unnerve Deven ... .).

(vii) *Still a two cigarette man* ? (Sent. 21)
(Disdainful, wants to belittle Deven.)

(viii) *Waiting for Deven to strike a match.* (Sent. 21)
(Wants to be served.)

(ix) *Murad said insolently, a full-fledged lecturer in a college, an important citizen of Mirpore, and still can't afford a whole packet of cigarettes. You seem to be where you were in your college days. What's the matter*? (Sent. 24-26)

(Murad has no consideration for the feelings of Deven. Tries to show off that he is better than Deven *i.e.* more successful in life. Tries to pose sincerity by asking, what the matter was? but does not mean it, that is clear from the next sentence uttered by him.)

(x) *Murad gave a yelp and a clap on Deven's shoulders,* '*Will I get a drink with my lunch*' ?

(The word 'yelp' suggests animal behaviour. Murad is inconsiderate to the core. Guessing Deven's financial condition he wants to force a drink from him.)

Murad exemplifies a man of flesh, boisterous, bullying and self-centred.

Contrary to her general practice Anita Desai uses more indefinite than definite articles in the passage. The generic nature of references points to the low self-esteem that Deven has and of which Murad takes full advantage. Deven has not learnt the important lesson, that goodness and power go together to make success.

Conclusion

Anita Desai's wizardry with words, is once again established by the study of the beginnings of her eight novels. Each novel presents a unique aspect of life, handled in the peculiar manner the theme demanded. Mostly psychological studies, the narration is aimed at delineating character through the objective world. She confirms to the tradition of the 'lyrical novel'. As Ralph Freedman says,

> "The lyrical novel (by contrast), seeks to combine man and world in a strangely inward, yet aesthetically objective form. This is not to say that lyrical writers are uninterested in the questions of human conduct that concern all fiction, but they view these questions in a different light. Their stages are not those on which men usually perform in the novel, but independent designs in which the awareness of men's experiences is merged with its objects. Rather than finding its 'Gestalt' in the limitation of an action, the lyrical novel absorbs action altogether and refashions it as a pattern of imagery."[26]

Cry the Peacock, the first novel of Anita Desai, is a portrayal of personality types. The writer does not reveal the names of the protagonists, but highlights the qualities possessed by them. Life is a matter of outlook, is the message suggested by the extensive use of the words *eye* and *see* in their different contexts.

This recognition is also supported by the prevailing views about the theme of the novel by different critics.

'The worlds of Maya (woman) and Gautam (the husband) are sharply contrasted in that both represent the extremities of feminine and masculine principle. Maya is seething in eros, manifested in her multi-dimensional projections of companionship, maternality, of Keatsian sensuousness; of her identification with petunias. Gautam on the other hand is an Apollonian, he is into form, order, discipline, career and logomachies.'[27]

"As a poetry novel it is truly extraordinary, both in the archetypal sense and in terms of numinosity and pathology."[28]

Desai's second novel, *Voices in the City* is based on contrasts, a gap between appearance and reality. Life is a matter of getting in the train or remaining outside it, of being an actor or an observer, of acceptance and rejection. The contrasts have been skilfully wrought in the scene from a railway platform, with the two brothers foregrounded representing the actor (Arun) and the observer (Nirode). As Jasbir Jain observes :

"The contrast is right in the beginning. Arun who is going abroad has been the father's favourite and has accepted routine, while Nirode loathes routine and wonders how can one spend one's lifetime on" something that does not matter.[29]

> "Arun and Nirode in their farewell meeting, hide their trueselves behind a facade of pretence. Nirode is aware of his love-hate relationship with Arun, of the envy which corrodes his very being, and is also aware that this is a final parting, yet the pretence is maintained that it is not so. Arun tells his brother" "I am sorry, 'now', to leave", to which Nirode replies "Liar...you're itching to start".[30]

The basic human qualities of emotional attachment are shared by both Arun and Nirode, but the direction each one chooses for himself, foretells the theme of the novel. As Usha Bande comments on, Nirode's lack of desire to undertake a journey as a pathological condition.

> "Nirode's inability to start a journey denotes the basic uncertainties in his temperament. He likes to sink comfortably into his effortless inevitability of the betrayed man. His real self is exiled and in its stead; there is the false 'I' operating. The centre of the realm of experience — the self — is absent. While the urge to start the journey assumes intermittently, almost pathological proportions, it is a mark of his lack of volition that he is powerless to act and set out on his journey."[31]

Bye-Bye Black Bird, Desai's third novel, describes the first day of Dev in England. The insight and minutiae of description amaze the careful reader. In the first five hundred words, the novelist deftly weaves the fine thread of an exotic design into the already tough and coloured cloth of Dev's Indian consciousness. In the words of R.S. Sharma,

> "*In Bye-Bye Black Bird*, the interaction between the locale and the individual acquires a new dimension, for the

tension here between the white locale and the immigrant black bird involves issues of alienation and accommodation that the immigrant has to confront in an alien and yet familiar world. The migratory blackbird is drawn to and repelled by the white England as its new habitat. Anita Desai captures this conflict in fictional terms through Dev."[32]

The next novel, *Where Shall We Go This Summer*, is another discovery in the ingenious craftsmanship of Anita Desai. A commonplace character and locale are the materials which evoke the sardonic grin of the author. The aim is to expose the hypocrisy and insignificance of man, juxtaposed with the great powers of nature. Life is a ridiculous waiting till a harmony between man and nature is struck. Atma Ram also supports this view.

"The novel seeks to unravel the inner mystery of life, to discover the energy that nourishes the spirit, and discards pettiness, horror and hypocrisy of every day life."[33]

The theme of the novel, 'Waiting', disclosed through a minor character, adds to the artistic sensibility of the author. A casual reader may perhaps miss the point altogether but the delightful pattern revealed by careful study fills one with wonder and admiration.

> "Are you waiting for someone?" she was occasionally asked by one of the children.... Sometimes she answered with a nod for it was true, she was always waiting.... I'm waiting, she agreed although for what, she could not tell : for the two halves of this grey egg-world to fall apart and burst into festival fireworks, a woman's seaweed hair or bloodstained feathers? For that would fling them all, tiny grey sand-lice, into icy force. But, till she came to it, she would live on, smothered by the endless damp, soft grey sand, and it seemed that these years of her life were dyed, coloured through and through with the colour of waiting. It was not a pure colour — it was tinged at, times with anxiety, at others with resignation or frenzy, patience, grimness, fear. But whatever its tint, its tone, it had seeped through her, flowed along every smallest capillary till she herself was turned a living monument to waiting."
>
> (*Where Shall We Go This Summer*? pp. 54-55)

Fire on the Mountain follows *Where Shall We Go This Summer* in ironical juxtaposition of the actual and the aesthetic. Nanda Kaul, a solitary figure in Kasauli is seething in her own aversion and self-imposed solitude. The heavenly bliss sought by her in Carignano, is actually a prison from where there is no escape, unless she redeems herself from her self-destructive attitude towards life. As Usha Bande comments,

> "Nanda Kaul in *Fire on the Mountain* is an old woman caught in the web of what Marten Buber calls, "self-contradictions," "the failure to work out and realise the inborn `Thou' and what meets it. 'Nanda Kaul is not aware of the split in her personality caused by the desire of the self to recoil from all contact and yet attempt to react out to the other."[34]

The writer scarcely tries to conceal her point of view. The contradictions inherent in the character of Nanda Kaul are evident from the first sentence of the novel.

> 'Nanda Kaul paused under the pine trees to take in their scented sibilance.'
>
> (*Fire on the Mountain*, p. 3)

Clear Light of Day, focuses on the disintegration of self from the physical reality of life. The lack of harmony between the world of nature and the human beings is apparent from the beginning passage. This lack of synchronization has been aptly observed by Jasbir Jain,

> "A whole man," Jung wrote in 'The Psychology of the unconscious,' however, knows that his bittered foe, or indeed a host of enemies, does not equal that one worst adversary the 'otherself' who dwells in his bosom." Bim in *Clear Light of Day*, as her anger seethes within her, as she walks up and down her rooms trying to conquer just this enemy. She realises that bitterness is beginning to engulf her relationship with others, there is more to wholeness than experience, or involvement or feeling. It implies the ability to rise above the limits of ego; not renunciation, withdrawal, asceticism, but cohesion of the disparate elements of one's being of emotion, reason and instinct.[35]

A Village by the Sea, intended for the younger reader, has a comparatively simple beginning, the contradictions, contrasts and irony present in the earlier novels are not obvious yet a careful study is rewarding. A study of the singular and plural nouns and the definite/indefinite articles lends an insight into the indirect observations on the rural consciousness, the difference in rural and urban world view and its outcome. In the opinion of Jasbir Jain,

> The *Village by the Sea* appeared in 1982. Intended for the younger reader, the novel has a deceptive simplicity but at a deeper level it continues the concerns of Desai's earlier novels. The thematic concerns and the narrative approach remain in large measure the ones she has used before, and these are the juxtaposition of value structures, the charm of the remote, the ability on part of time to crystallize issues and explorations of relationships.[36]

In the story it is not the individual, but the individual in society which is important, rather, it is a study of a particular economic group.

The eighth novel, *In Custody* again is a probe into personality traits. Deven Sharma the protagonist of the novel is in his own custody, that is to say, the reasons for his failure in life are the flaws in his personality. Deven's gentleness and non-assertive nature is the cause of his undoing. Usha Bande observes the same in her book.

> "The novel unfolds the story of credulous and disingenuous Deven Sharma, who is swayed by an idea of creating a work of his lifetime, but is, unfortunately, defeated by his own helplessness.... The prime characteristics of Deven that attract our attention are his helplessness, humility, suffering and nobility."[37]

The novels when viewed as the work of one person, do reveal some common features of style.

Anita Desai prefers simple words to polysyllabic words. A discreet mixture of Saxon and Latin words give her English a native touch. Although writing about human psyche she uses more concrete nouns than abstract. This is to eliminate the 'disjunction of self and world'. As a result of this — Her writing gains in authenticity, since man's two halves the subjective and the objective make a whole. For vividness and visibility she includes adjectives, referring to physical and psychological states. The narrative voice is mirrored in evaluative epithets.

A large number of adverbs of time, place, direction and degree give her writing a palpable quality — and the adverbs of manner throw light on the personalities of the characters, so as to render their total image for immediate apprehension.

A judicous use of disjuncts, adjuncts and conjuncts clarifies the contrasts and juxtapositions of which her writing is full.

A balanced use of transitive and intransitive verbs adds speed to the progression of images, which are created in order to dramatize an inner conflict and symbolize it objectively through a situation or object. The transitive verbs give the reader an impression of movement and activity and thus add liveliness to the description.

Anita Desai prefers complex sentences to simple ones. The passages have approximately a ratio of 1:8 between simple and complex sentences. The complexity arises due to subordination and coordination both. Anita Desai favours non-finite clauses *i.e.*, infinitive with to, infinitive without to, ing-participle and ed-participle. The use of non-finite clauses is a mark of careful writing. These clauses result in compactness and hence aid fluent reading.

Relative clauses and adverb clauses are frequently used for pre-modification and post-modification. Anticipatory clauses also frequently used, serve the purpose of orientation and add suspense to the writing.

An interesting feature of her style is the use of articles. She makes stinting use of generic references, but far from attaching insignificance these serve as foregrounding devices which make explicit the intentions and inclinations of the characters. These also serve as a scale to measure the weightage the writer assigns a particular character or idea *e.g.*, unlike the other opening passages, the one in, *In Custody*, has the maximum number of generic references. On scrutiny it is realized that Deven's personality has been depicted lacking in specificity and direction : a lack of self-confidence leading others to underestimate him.

A well-known feature of Desai's style is, her use of figures of speech. Metaphors and similes, personification, pathetic fallacy, alliteration and assonance are very common, but the towering figure employed by Desai is that of irony which serves as the leit-motif in almost all her writing. Anita Desai in the garb of beautiful words and phrases has tried to probe deep into human psyche. The findings range from amusing to laughable, from laughable to ridiculous and from ridiculous to pathetic. Seldom does she give vent to anger, because that might prove to be destructive, instead she leaves the final word to the reader. Perhaps this is her way of purging life of its baseness.

A fondness for some special images needs to be mentioned here. Images based on light and flight are Desai's favourites. *Clear Light of Day*, *Bye-Bye Black Bird* and *The Village by the Sea*, all have their temporal setting in the morning at sunrise. In *Cry the Peacock* and *Fire on the Mountain* the sun plays an important role. In all five novels listed above light and sun explain the leit-motif. Although there is no direct reference to light in *Where Shall We Go This Summer* and *In Custody*, the story begins in daylight and an exclusive mention of diurnal activities associates them with light.

Two titles, *Bye-Bye Black Bird* and *Cry the Peacock*, directly depend on bird imagery, whereas birds are symbolically very prominent in *Voices in the City*, *Clear Light of Day*, and *Fire on the Mountain*. There is a detailed mention of sea birds in *The Village by the Sea*. Aerial activity is foregrounded by the description of the monsoon in *Where Shall We Go This Summer*? and by 'a march wind' in *In Custody*.

Another recurring image is that of boundaries or limits. In every passage limits are suggested by words like horizon (3), fringe, edge, lane lengths and limiter adjective, less.

Anita Desai like Jane Austin paints on a limited canvas, this awareness is reflected in her words. Parataxis, ellipsis and parenthesis are other devices employed freely. They save the narration from excessive formality, retaining naturalness of expression. Parenthesis can be termed as asides with the reader, a kind of intimacy resulting in happy rapport. Parenthesis also serves the purpose of explanation, modification, comment and reflection.[38]

For cohesion, Anita Desai takes recourse to lexical repetition, the use of pronouns and definite article. Besides these the underlying idea is a strong unifying link between paragraphs. A careful arrangement of paragraphs is another distinctive feature which is very evident from the organisation of material. Despite being a part of a bulk, the beginnings are all self-contained units. The premise overtly stated or hinted in the introductory lines is verified at the end summing up the logic and sequence in short, well defined sentences. For *e.g.*, *Voices in the City*, begins with a general comment on the train. The ending paragraph in the passage also has a comment on the general activities associated with the train in addition to the parting of the two brothers, which has been foregrounded in the middle part. Likewise, in *Fire on the Mountain* the funny choices of Nanda Kaul stated in the beginning are summed up in very brief statements in the last paragraph. The other novels too follow the same pattern. As Herbert Read says,

> "There is about good writing a visual actuality. It exactly reproduces what we should metaphorically call the contour of our thought. The metaphor is for once exact : thought has a contour or shape.... The writer has towards his materials, words, the same relation that an artist say a modeller has towards his material clay. The paragraph is a plastic mass and it takes its shape from the thought it has to express : its shape is the thought."[39]

This somehow is entirely applicable to the writings of Anita Desai. The intricate detail and patterning are beyond the limits of human contrivances. The only explanation is an instinctive understanding of relationship between language and thought.

REFERENCES

1. Quoted from, Geoffery N. Leech & Michael H. Short, *Style in Fiction* (Longman : London and New York, 1981), p. 3.
2. *Ibid.*, p. 5.
3. J. Warburg, *Some Aspects of Style* : The teaching of English. Studies in Communication 3 ed. (Randolf Quirk & A.H. Smith, 1959), pp. 47-55.
4. Leech & Short, p. 13.
5. *Ibid.*, p. 4.
6. *Ibid.*, p. 5.
7. David Lodge, *Language of Fiction* (London : Routledge and Kegan Paul, 1970), p. 28.
8. *Ibid.*, p. 78.
9. Leech and Short, p. 179.

10. *Ibid.*, p. 3.
11. *Ibid.*, pp. 75-80.
12. Herbert Read, *English Prose Style* (Ludhiana : Lyall Book Depot, 1968).
13. Leech and Short, p. 226.
14. Roger Fowler, *Linguistic Criticism* (Oxford : Oxford University Press, 1986), p. 164.
15. Randolph Quirk and Sidney Greenbaum, *A University Grammar of English* (London : Longman, 1973), p. 200.
16. Geoffery N. Leech, *A Linguistic Guide to English Poetry* (London : Longman, 1969), p. 158.
17. Anita Desai, *Cry the Peacock* (1963, Delhi : Vision Books, 1983), pp. 5-6.
18. Anita Desai, *Voices in the City* (Delhi : Orient Paperbacks, 1965), pp. 5-6.
19. Anita Desai, *Bye-Bye Black Bird* (Delhi : Vision Books, 1985), pp. 5-6.
20. David Lodge, *Language of Fiction* (London : Routledge and Kegan Paul, 1970), p. 39.
21. Anita Desai, *Where Shall We Go This Summer*? (Delhi : Orient Paperbacks, 1975), pp. 7-8.
22. Anita Desai, *Fire on the Mountain* (Middlesex : Penguin Publications, 1977), pp. 3-4.
23. Anita Desai, *Clear Light of Day* (New Delhi : Allied Publishers, 1980), pp. 1-2.
24. Anita Desai, *A Village by the Sea* (New Delhi : Allied Publishers, 1982), pp. 7-8.
25. Anita Desai, *In Custody* (London : Penguin Books, 1984), pp. 9-10.
26. Ralph Freedman, *The Lyrical Novel* (Princeton : Princeton University Press, New Jersey, 1963), p. 2.
27. Som P. Sharma, Kamal N. Awasthi, "Anita Desai's *Cry the Peacock* : A vindication of the Feminine", in *Perspectives on Anita Desai*, ed., R.K. Shrivastava (Ghaziabad : Vimal Prakashan, 1984), p. 140.
28. *Ibid.*, p. 138.
29. Jasbir Jain, *Stairs to the Attic, the Novels of Anita Desai* (Jaipur : Printwell, 1987), p. 22.
30. *Ibid.*, p. 43.
31. Usha Bande, *The Novels of Anita Desai* (New Delhi : Prestige Books, 1988), p. 77.
32. R.S. Sharma, *Anita Desai* (Liverpool : Lucas Publications, 1981), p. 69.

33. Atma Ram, *The Journal of Indian Writing in English*, Vol. 9, No. 1, Ed. G.S. Balarama Gupta (Annamalai University, Jan. 1981), p. 80.
34. Usha Bande, p. 90.
35. Jasbir Jain, p. 126.
36. *Ibid.*, p. 25.
37. Usha Bande, p. 154.
38. F.A. Inamdar, "Anita Desai's Prose Style", in *Perspectives on Anita Desai*, p. 95.
39. Herbert Read, *English Prose Style* (Ludhiana : Lyall Book Depot, 1968), p. 61.

3

FORM AND STRUCTURE

A STUDY OF THE FOUR MAJOR NOVELS —

CRY THE PEACOCK, VOICES IN THE CITY, FIRE ON THE MOUNTAIN, AND WHERE SHALL WE GO THIS SUMMER ?

Rene Welleck and Austin Warren, define the terms 'form' and 'structure' in the following manner :

"Form would include all linguistic elements by which contents are expressed."

"The manner in which materials acquire aesthetic efficacy, may be called structure."

"Structure is a concept including both context and form, so far they are organised for aesthetic purposes. The work of art is, then considered as a whole, system of signs, or structure of signs, serving a specific aesthetic purpose."[1]

Keeping in view the above definitions, the four novels of Anita Desai have been analysed with reference to the linguistic elements as an expression of the context, arranged in a systematic manner, for a special aesthetic purpose.

At the turn of the century it was realized by many writers, prominent among whom are Andre Gide, Conrad, Herman Hesse, James Joyce, Virginia Woolf and Henry James, that the traditional technique of novel writing, such as "point of view and narrative plot can be utilized not only to produce a likely world of action but to find formal analogues for a private world".[2] Irwing Howe expresses the same idea as follows :

> "In the past hundred years we have had a special kind of literature. We call it modern and distinguish it from the merely contemporary, for where the contemporary refers to time, the modern refers to sensibility and style, and where the contemporary is a term of neutral reference, the modern is a term of critical placement and judgement."[3]

The novels of Anita Desai are "modern" in the very sense of the word suggested above. Meena Belliappa writes in her book, Anita Desai : A study of her Fiction : "The focus of interest has shifted from girlish romance to a more complex search for value in human relationship."[4] "The focus of interest lies in the portrayal of states of mind rather than holding up the mirror to society. The fiction tends to be structured vertically. The effort is to capture the atmosphere of the mind and directly involve the reader in the flow of a particular consciousness. A marked leaning towards such introversion is seen in Anita Desai's writing."[5]

Form and Structure, in the novels of Anita Desai, 'take the shape of an exquisitely designed tapestry''.[6] ''The story and the novel, the idea and the form, are the needle and the thread'',[7] says Henry James, "the cultivation of this success, the study of this exquisite process form to my taste, is the beginning and the end of the art of the novelist. They are his inspiration, his despair, his reward, his torment, his delight. It is here in very truth that he competes with life; it is here that he competes with his brother the painter in his attempt to render the look of things, the look that conveys their meaning, to catch the colour, the relief, the expression, the surface, the substance of the human spectacle."[8]

The novels of Anita Desai reveal her unique world view, but at the same time confirm to the existing tendencies in modern fiction. Her novels are technical innovations which "combine features of both novel and lyrical poetry and shift the reader's attention from men and events to a formal design".[9] She herself prefers the word 'pattern' to plot.

"I prefer the word 'pattern' to 'plot' as it sounds-more natural and even better, if I dare use it, is Hopkin's, word 'inscape' —

while 'plot' sounds arbitrary heavy-handed and artificial, all that I wish to avoid."[10]

Ralph Freedman in his book the lyrical novel has enumerated the typical features of modern novels based on the inner drama of human psyche. He calls these novels, lyrical novels. Anita Desai's main concern in writing too is the quest of truth. She writes,

> "Writing to me is a process of discovering the truth — the truth that is nine-tenths of the iceberg that lies submerged beneath one-tenth visible portion we call reality. Writing is my way of plunging to the depths and exploring this underlying truth. All my writing is an effort to discover, to underline and convey the true significance of things."[11]

For Anita Desai, it is not the theme, but the inner and outer rhythms of human psyche which are all important.

"My novels don't have themes — at least not till they are finished, published or read, do I see any theme. While writing, I follow my instinct, I follow flashes of insight, I veer away from or even fight anything that threatens to distort or destroy this insight, and somehow come to the end and look back to see the pattern of footprints on the sand."[12]

> According to Irwing Howe : "The modernists anticipate the preoccupation with psychic inwardness, by means of which the self is transformed into a cosmic centre and mover, as this will later become characteristic of certain modernist writers, but they still seek to relate this preoccupation to transcendental values, if not sources, in the external world. For them the universe is still alert, still the active transmitter of spiritual signs".[13]

In the light of the above observation, Anita Desai is a modernist who shares some common features with other prominent writers of our times. Some salient features peculiar to this kind of writing have been discussed in detail by Ralph Freedman :[14]

"The main figure in the novel is the symbolic hero, a passive purveyor of visions, who in quest of meaning of life absorbs the external world and mirrors it in all its multitudinous manifestations. He is also an aesthetic image who wears the novelist's mask and thus through his contradictory self, in the end, produces a picture of a unified or total self.

This romanticised hero in his quest, reaches a point of recognition which enables him to become an aesthetic abstraction of the universal.

The transcendental or romanticised hero reflects a spiritual image of man's relation to his universe, rising from subjective sensibility and moving to a formal presentation.

The telescopic self of the hero, operates through physical objects which serve as the catalyst, leading him on to hallucinations and dreams, expressed through a succession of image scenes.

The method of ironic juxtaposition is applied for a heightened expression of feeling. The prose poems can take up different forms, they can be ironic or passionate, cruelly realistic, loftily symbolic, allegorical or parabolic.

The past life of the protagonists plays an important role, as the present consciousness of the characters is a result of their past experiences. Therefore, the plot moves with the modulations of memory. The hero becomes a wanderer through space and time.

These novels are psychological dramas, surfacing an inner conflict, through aesthetic objectivity. The poet novelist mirrors himself in the theme, and at the same time remains detached, till he is able to produce a spiritual self-image. This intrinsic relationship between all animate and inanimate objects, becomes the sole subject of the lyrical novelist. In short, lyrical novels are long prose poems, based on subjective objectivity, expressed through a progression of images in which the symbolic hero or the protagonist is the poet's mask, engaged in self-analysis, 'his quest which leads him to a moment of recognition, and transcends the temporal and causal, unifying the individual self with the infinite or universal self'."

For Anita Desai too "writing is not an act of deliberation, reason, and choice. It is a matter of instinct, silence and waiting. It is the movement of the wing one tries to capture not the bird. That is, it is the image that matters, the symbol, the myth, the feat of associating them, of relating them, of constructing with them. Whether one does this in one's native or in a foreign tongue is not essentially important. It can be done in any language at all; only it must be done spontaneously, compulsively, subconsciously,

'Only connect'. That is what a writer's existence is all about — he connects, he connects, all the time he connects. It is a process that does indeed employ language but also transcends it."[15]

In the four novels selected for this aspect of study, the approach of the novelist may vary from novel to novel, but the basic framework of each, fits in the criteria for a lyrical novel like pieces in a jigsaw-puzzle.

Anita Desai has adopted a controlled method of stream of consciousness. 'Internal narration'[16], a point of view within a character's consciousness, manifesting his or her feelings about and evaluations of the events and characters of the story. It is used extensively in *Cry the Peacock* and to a limited extent in *Voices in the City*. Major part of these writings include 'free-indirect-discourse',[17] indicating an internal perspective, in which the subjective feelings of protagonists are transformed into third person narration and are interwoven with, and framed by the author's account of the character's inner state.

The first novel of Anita Desai,[18] can almost be taken as a model of a poetry novel.

The chief protagonist is Maya, who wears the poet narrators mask and portrays the poetic vision through her public monologues.

The plot moves with the modulations of memory. The scenes from Maya's childhood alternate with her present condition and her concern for the future, tattooed with the albino astrologer's predictions. Maya is a passive purveyor of visions whose awareness of self is merged with objects surrounding her. The novel has hardly any action, and the reader gets the feeling of movement in the plot due to the progression of images, one after the other.

The novel begins with an image scene, in which the names of the characters are not revealed right till the end of the chapter, and the reader is unconsciously drawn to the inner world of Maya's psyche. The symbolic self-portrait of Maya is painted step by step by the juxtaposition of other characters and scenes like Gautam, Lila, Pom, Maya's father, Gautam's mother, sister, the image scenes *viz.*, the scene of the meeting with the albino astrologer, Cabaret dancers, the dinner parties and storm scene in the end, which intensify Maya's inner state of turmoil.

Maya as the symbolic hero, absorbs the animate and the inanimate world around her. She, as the mask of the author deforms these experiences, in order to mirror an aesthetic image.

The anithetical technique adopted, is clearly visible in the two different worlds, in which the consciousness of Maya vacillates, *i.e.*, the dream world of her childhood and the world of solid reality of Gautam's house and family. Maya describes her childhood days :

> "The world is like a toy specially made for me, painted in my favourite colours, set moving to my favourite tune." (*Cry the Peacock*, p. 36)

A doting father, who looked after this dream-child Maya, is remembered with special tenderness.

> "He has looked after me alone and his beam is especially tender, his attention especially loving. I think, that he is like a silver oak himself, with his fine silver white hair brushed smoothly across his bronzed scalp." (p. 39)

Maya's after-marriage life is a complete change. Her husband Gautam holds :

> "Reality and idealism are one and the same thing. Life is not a matter of distinguishing between the two but of reconciling them." (pp. 20-21)

Gautam's mother is entirely different from Maya's father.

> ".... like some busy rhinoceros charging through the forest, to her dispensary, or her creche, or her workshop for the blind, the disabled, the unemployed." (p. 47)

Maya's married life is juxtaposed with that of Lila and Pom, the self-contented beings, representing compromise in life.

> "....what hated me was not a remembrance of Leila bitter, but a memory of Leila resigned. Had she raged, revolted, I should have rushed to her now." (p. 59)

> "It was natural, afterthoughts of Leila, to turn down a line of friends, sift them through my mind and come to Pom, the pink, plump, pretty Pom who did not speak of fate, who had never been ill, or overworked or bitter." (p. 60)

Maya is searching for the right coloured sari for that day in her cupboard, while thinking about her friends. In this symbolic scene, in the end, she gives up the search, torn by her internal conflict and quest for peace and solace.

> "I ceased to hunt then, ceased to plan, and merely laid my face into those cool cloths, odorous with camphor and lavender, that recalled mountain waters to me, ferns, and nights full of stars, for I found myself alone with them after all. There was not one of my friends who could act as an anchor any more, and to whomsoever I turned for reassurance, betrayed me now." (p. 64)

The very delicate vibrations of Maya's thought dominate the novel.

> "Values were distorted in that macabre half light with its altering tints at an hour when those values could have been all important. What was true? What was lasting? What to believe in? What reject?" (p. 86)

Maya has been shown as the aesthetic abstraction of the universal self.

> "Lying here in the dark? he said, and drew a finger down my cheek. Fall, fall, long fall into the soft velvet well of the primordium, of original instinct, of first formed love." (p. 11)

Maya reflects a spiritual image of man's relation to his universe.

> "It was not only for his presence, his love that I longed for but mainly for the life that would permit me to touch him, feel his flesh and hair, hold and then tighten my hold on him. And not on Gautam alone, but on all the pulsating world around him, from the freize of stars silently exploding in the summer sky to the faintly fluttering owls making covert hidden love in the crotch of the fig tree — All that suggested life, and the great entrancing world to me who was doomed not to live." (p. 102)

Just before she carries out her unspoken decision, Maya has the experience of oneness with nature almost transcendental in nature.

> "I continued to mount, step by step, to the roof, looking up to see the evening sky lowering itself to descend upon me till suddenly when I had burst out into the open we were one — the blue intensity and I." (p. 205)

This spiritual experience is the natural outcome of an inner conflict, which resolves itself gradually, through a series of probes and questionings and recognition of truth from time to time.

"Here lay the catalysis of my unrest I had grown too involved." (p. 67)

"I entered a new vista of knowledge. I forced myself into believing that I could see now what must be the reason for my hating it so, for my hating it so, for Gautam's spurning it — visible to our subconscious only." (p. 106)

Maya detaches herself in order to reach this knowledge.

"Murder

Shocked as though I had truly found a blemish in my unscarred skin. I drew away from the mirror with a shudder I could no longer bear to see that clear, ignorant and insane face, and looked away." (p. 106)

Anita Desai not only follows the trends of lyrical novel but even makes the protagonist use the very words which express this lyrical process.

Freedman says, "This process of telescoping self and world is based in the main on the idealistic epistemology of the time."[19]

Maya reverberates the idea :

"My suddenly sobered mind affirmed it a certainty, as the telescope affirms the certainty of the physical substance of these mysterious lights in the night sky, the planets. No fairy tales those, but proven." (p. 20)

In the words of Freedman again.

"The hero as an aesthetic image of nature leads to the technique of mirroring. Since the self is the point at which inner and outer worlds are joined, the hero's mental picture reflects the universe of sensible encounters as an image."[20] This very subjective process is described by Maya objectively.

'I saw my body detach itself from it and float away, to rest upon the dim mirror where I could gaze upon it from a cool distance I studied it absorbed.' (p. 105)

'The unique personage of the poetic hero (Maya) moves in worlds transformed by her own hallucinations; her temperament, in her deformations lies the unique reality.'[21]

"Swiftly I turn, swiftly I run. I feel my heart throbbing madly.

Why?

> Wild horse, white horse, galloping up paths of stone, flying away into the distance, the wild hills. The heights, the dizzying heights of my mountains, towering, tapering, edged with cliff-edges founded on rock. Fall, fall gloriously fall to the bed of racing rivers, foaming seas. Horrid arms and legs tentacles thrashing, blood flowing, eyes glazing. Storm-storm at sea, at land! fury. Whip lash, Fly furiously. Danger! Danger! The warning rings and echoes, from far, far, far. Run and hide, run and hide if you can miserable fool! Ha, ha, fool, fool, fool." (pp. 180-81)

Maya redefines love and life in her own way. The lyrical point of view in this particular novel is the justification of the protagonists 'I'. Till the very end, she wished to be loved and understood.

> "I was overcome with a desperate timidity, begging him once more to answer to come and meet me half-way, in my own world, not merely demand of me, brusquely to join me in his, which, however safe, was so very drab and no longer offered me security.
>
> Had he done so, all might have been quite different.
>
> But he did not. Less than that, he retreated to the outposts of his flat civilization and asked vaguely, half-interestedly, 'Toto? who was that?"
>
> The words were as grim as any death sentence absolute and unredeemable." (p. 198)

The poet narrator successfully justifies the emnations of Maya's consciousness. Because of Gautam's half-deadness to the living world, which his dry brain (p. 195) was incapable of sensing, Maya feels justified in her decision. The objects, scenes, characters, all exist in the novel as image figures to objectify and dramatize the protagonists point of view. The atmosphere of subjective objectivity so skilfully created makes the novel a work of art.

Voices in the City[22], is a lyrical novel with a difference. The protagonists 'I' is not represented by a single person but consists of three individuals, Nirode, Monisha and Amla who present a divided point of view, but combine towards the end. The book has been divided into four sections. The first three deal with the hero's quest, while the fourth is attempted as a spiritual generalization, based on all that has been related in the previous pages. The plot oscillates between past and present, childhood and concern for future play a meaningful role in the present lives of the protagonists.

Nirode in the first part of the book is the editor of a magazine who wants to cast off all his family connections, contrary to Maya, who was haunted by an idyllic childhood, Nirode wants to get rid of his attachment for his mother whom he believes to be leading a life of disgrace. He tells Sonny :

> "And you set about teaching me what to accept and what to reject — after I've thrown off every stinking undergarment of family fortune and family." (*Voices in the City*, p. 25)

Nirode is in search of a meaning of life, and a life of detachment, but at every step feels thwarted and torn by an internal conflict.

> "No. The newspaper carries the writer further and further into the impersonal, it only follows the you. The You is everything in the news. There is never an I. It is the I that interests me now." (p. 32)

Juxtaposed with Nirode's search for truth are the portraits of Sonny, the once upon a time rich landlord's son, Jit Nair, whose wife has eloped, with her lover David the foreigner who lives a hand to mouth existence, trying to understand India, Dharma, a queer painter. All these figures have their own personal handicaps, but pose to lead normal lives.

Nirode is a rebel. He symbolises the contradictions in human nature and as a passive purveyor of visions, wishes to rise higher, towards an ideal self.

> "For one drink following upon a day of such intensity had made Nirode transparent, revealed inside him the arterial network that now spread and grew on a plane slightly above that of Calcutta's tumultuous roofscape, but attached to it by countless wires telegraph poles, chimneys, pigeon-roosts — one vast tangled net of the Bengali loquaciousness, the Bengali's quick emotion and fluency, his natural anarchism, his imbalance and inconsistencies, his dark and demoniac dreams that grovelled mostly in the grossness of the city, its shapeless, colourless and grim old houses and slums, then heaved up, like the radio aerials and pigeon-roosts

> that collected the fuzz of smog on the roofs, and now and then rose and fled like a scattering of mother-of-pearl pigeons into a forbidding sky. He spoke with conceit and malice, he disregarded his companions with fine philosophic detachment, then noisily crashed into their midst again. He boasted of his various wild experiences, declaring them unique in one of his social class, little realizing it was the city that had thrust them upon him inexorably. Then with unconscious candour, he wondered aloud what to make of it all." (p. 22)

All the subjective qualities, listed in the passage have their objective counterparts, *viz.*, the arterial network in Nirode has been associated with the countless wires, telegraph poles, chimneys, pigeon roosts etc. Nirode's demoniac dreams, natural anarchism, imbalance, inconsistencies are paralleled with shapeless, colourless grim old houses and slums.

A succession of images to externalise the internal, to make abstract concrete, is a distinguishing feature of lyrical novels and this novel abounds in images and image scenes serving as formal analogues for a private world. In fact the entire novel is a network of interlocking images.

The story begins with Nirode, followed by Monisha's first person account and public monologues, further joined by the experiences of Amla. Overlapping ruminations are apparent. Monisha mirrors the personality and experiences of Nirode, and Amla does the same for Monisha. In a lyrical novel the protagonists absorb objects and persons in order to achieve aesthetic objectivity. Nirode, Amla and Monisha, three personages, engaged in search of meaning of life cope with it in their own way, confront the moment of recognition, and form their own resolutions which in the end merge with the universal.

The lyrical process makes the protagonists distort the universe, or dissolve it into hallucinations or dream, to reveal the infinite and the organic. Nirode, wishes to brush up with the past but is reminded, or rather gripped by it in his dream.

> "Into Nirode's sleep the bright birds of the past came serenely winging, and the wide gestures of their wings ushered into his sleep the gemmed loveliness of a holiday home of his childhood...." (p. 26)

Thinking of the empty miserable life of Bengali women, Monisha is lost in hallucination, when she sees the 'Bleeding Heart' Doves in the zoo.

> "What does it all mean? Why are lives such as these lived? At their conclusion, what solution, what truth falls into the waiting palm of one's hand, the still pit of one's heart?
>
> Here is the answer — here, here, here, Look. I will scream. I cannot believe — but here it is. Look through these bars, into this cage of doves — look, look at the terrible answer...." (p. 121)

Amla experiences perfect happiness in the presence of Dharma. She is translucent with joy and overflowing with a sense of love and reward (p. 210), but in her subconscious, is scared of losing it, of being cheated.

> "At night in her dreams, Amla believed that they were former models turned into white birds by Dharma, warning and scolding her in their harsh broken voices." (p. 211)
>
> "There were moments when Amla feared to touch a paint brush, feeling it might take wing and swoop out of the window, or the ring on her finger, half expecting to see a caterpillar crawl out of the Tibetan turquoise." (p. 212)

The leitmotif of the novel is journey. The novel begins with an image scene, the very first line of which describes the train in subjective as well as objective terms. The symbolic vision includes journey at every step. Nirode, the chief protagonist, always connects his ideas and experiences with train and journey.

> "Nirode groaned, 'I'd never go, David I never shall'. I pack my bags. 'I arrive at the station,' and when I have one foot in the train, I hesitate. That's my undoing — this lack of faith and this questioning. I just stand and watch the train rush off, leaving me behind like a ghost in a bloody nightmare."
>
> David : "I find the ticket alone answers all my questions, reassures one completely".
>
> Nirode : "Ah, do you? For me, all tickets are marked with question marks. That is all I ever find on them." (p. 39)

The recognition of truth has also been described in terms of a journey.

> 'He wondered if man did not lose something of himself in this quarrel with his instincts, and if, in being a victor, there was not also a part of him — a part that had been remote, curious and unique — that was vanquished. And if it was not better therefore to be — to be — what? What can a man be if he is not a freak ? If he journeys, his body and mind will suffer expense, and perhaps the moral of it all is not to avoid the expense, but merely to make the journey worth the expense.' (p. 225)

Amla on the other hand feels weak and exhausted when confronted with truth.

> "A combination of all these revelations and inspirations filled her, expanded her, made her rise and float, and on its drift she left the house, feeling as emptied out, frangible and exhausted as if a high fever had drained her." (p. 231)

But she also learns the need for continuity in life from birds, which serve as a catalyst, which changes the finite self of Amla into an infinite aesthetic self. A part of the chain of life.

> "These birds they stay in the trees inspite of all those crowds around them, all that shouting and jumping and pushing. They don't give up their trees. They are not afraid. Isn't that strange?" (p. 232)

At the races Amla realises that the world cheers the winner, one who falls and dies is soon forgotten. It is life and living which matters not death.

Monisha on the other hand feels defeated.

> "I am turned into a woman who keeps a diary. I do not like a woman who keeps a diary. Traceless, meaningless, uninvolved, does this not amount to non-existence, please?" (p. 140)

It is the recognition of losing the battle of instinct, the essential human in her, which leads her to her final resolution.

> "These people know and feel something I do not, they are all nodding in agreement with the singer, they understand what she is singing to them. If I won a war over the mind, then they lost a war to their instincts,

> and it seems my victory has less value than their loss." (p. 239)

As Novelist suggests, in a lyrical novel, imagination transforms nature from a mechanism into a poetic whole. The artist thus renders an image of infinite nature and his own infinite self, the symbolic hero is the passive instrument of this process.[23]

Monisha's sense of loss on not being able to have the primeval feelings of love and involvement, is a glimpse of the ideal self she aspires to attain, but fails.

> In the end of the novel, Nirode and Amla together present a picture of the transcendental or symbolic hero who is the aesthetic abstraction of the universal. The contradictory point of views are all merged into the ideal self. Calcutta is no more a city stirring with its own marsh bred, monster life that like an ogre kept one eye open through sleep and waking (p. 41), but it is the city which is ever bowed in worship to the *Great Kali*, the mother of all. *Kali*, who is reality and illusion, the world and Maya is one (p. 256).

This awareness of the universal by the protagonists is the point of highest concentration in the novel. The quest is over, the journey of life is no more reckless but directed by an unseen power, omnipresent, omniscient and omnipotent. The animate and the inanimate are combined into a harmonious whole.

This drama of the voices, with the great palpable city in the background, reveals all the features of a lyrical novel. The passive hero, action replaced by perception, the quest for the meaning in life, the inner conflict in the protagonists to realize an ideal self, the romanticized hero reflecting a spiritual image of man's relation with the universe, expressed through symbols and images including both subjective and the objective worlds.

"A decisive difference between the conventional narrative and the lyrical novel is the treatment of the outer world. In the first, it is placed beyond both writer and reader, imposing between them and the theme. In lyrical mode such a world is conceived not as a universe in which men display their actions, but as a poet's vision, fashioned as a design. The world is reduced to a lyrical point of view, the equivalent of the poet's 'I', the lyrical self."[24]

In *Fire on the Mountain*,[25] the self-destructive fire in the heart and mind of Nanda Kaul, juxtaposed with the bare physical surroundings caused by forest fires, decides the lyrical point of view.

> ...he stopped and kept behind while Nanda Kaul, slit-eyed burned on the knoll. (*Fire on the Mountain*, p. 5)

The poetic design consists of Nanda Kaul a recluse by circumstance, Raka, a recluse by choice, and Ila Das a born recluse, because of her physical handicaps.

The setting is the symbolic house, called Carignano, which stands alone on a knoll, a meeting place for the three protagonists. The sets are combined both by explicit statements and implicit imagery. Only one more figure interacts with the three main protagonists, that is Ramlal. This sparseness of characters, matches with the sparseness in vegetation.

Nanda Kaul is the passive purveyor of visions, who had chosen the house to find rest and relief from the mad world of duties and obligations. Through her, the poet narrator makes explicit her poetic vision. Nanda Kaul, as the symbolic hero, distorts the world in order to create an aesthetic image.

> "It was the place, and the time of life, that she had wanted and prepared for all her life." (p. 3)
>
> "What pleased and satisfied her so, here at Carignano, was its barrenness. This was the chief virtue of all Kasauli of course — its starkness." (p. 4)

Kasauli, a hill station, is presented as a barren, dry, unattractive place, surrounded by scenes of past and present forest fires, and always threatened with a new one. Nanda Kaul's choice of a house, at such a place, becomes the focal point of this dry and burnt landscape, which in fact, symbolises the inner self of the protagonist.

A certain ambiguity of purpose prevails, which is again a characteristic of lyrical novels. This ambiguity is caused by ironical tones adopted to depict the conflict, between the real and the fleeing, escaping self of Nanda Kaul. Nanda Kaul wishes to break up with the past, but the past continuously impinges on her privacy and distracts her vision.

The protagonist's quest is represented symbolically by a lyrical progression, produced by elaborate picture scenes. The whole novel is interspersed with references to the past, in the form of the history of Carignano, life at Nanda Kaul's husband, the vice-chancellor's house, scenes from Nanda Kaul's childhood, history of Raka's parents, the history of Ila Das.

The present is mainly represented by Raka, her exploits and adventures, in direct juxtaposition with the experiences of Nanda Kaul and Ila Das, who are three generations removed from her.

The concept of subjective objectivity followed by Anita Desai is present in this novel also. The experiences of Nanda Kaul, who is in search of a total self, are arranged in a pattern of imagery. This pattern includes both human beings and objects, and are manifestations of the acting thought. Prominent images include Carignano — for seclusion, Kasauli — barrenness, starkness; History of Carignano — the loneliness misery of life, especially of lonely and unmarried women; Postman — animal existence; school boy — life of instincts; Ramlal — servant endowed with a kind and gentle heart; life of Tara-failure of social life; and life at Vice Chancellor's house — duties and obligations; appearances; letters, messages, telephones — the outside world with which Nanda Kaul wished to have no connection; Eagle — Nanda Kaul's aspirations for attaining higher self, the club-vanity and hollowness of a life of appearances; insects, lizards, crickets, cicadas — low self-esteem for herself and Raka; the climb to the monkey point — difference in age.

These are but a few listed. A single image may symbolise many things at the same time.

Raka is the catalyst in this novel. She leads Nanda Kaul to the discovery of truth. In a lyrical novel, the protagonists wear the mask of the poet narrator. For the purpose of dramatic juxtaposition, the hero detaches himself from the scene of action, absorbs the action, and through the process of perception, mirrors it to create an ideal world. Here in this novel, Nanda Kaul is only an observer, while Raka enacts the moral point of view in symbolic gestures. Raka does not change herself because :

"If Nanda Kaul was a recluse out of vengeance for a

> long life of duty and obligations her great grand-daughter was a recluse by nature, by instinct she had not arrived at the condition by a long route of rejection and sacrifice, she was born to it simply." (p. 48)

Raka is often referred to as an insect, a cricket, a pet insect (pp. 39, 42, 45 and 54), which suggest that she was completely at home with nature. Unlike Nanda Kaul, she does not dream of orchards in Kashmir (p. 93), but is happy to indulge in the hallucination of becoming a ship wrecked hero.

> "I'm ship wrecked, Raka exulted. I'm ship wrecked and alone. She clung to a rock — my boat, alone in my boat on the sea, she sang." (p. 61)

If Nanda Kaul's quest for ideal self spelt calm and peace, for Raka it was complete oneness with the elements of nature. She is ecstatic to set the forest on fire. It is doubtful whether she was left unscathed.

> "There was a scratching at the window that turned to a tapping, then a drumming, Nani, Nani, whispered Raka, shivering and crouching in the lily -bed peeping over the sill. Look Nani, I have set the forest on fire." (p. 145)

This novel is the story of two persons. As Freedman says, 'The relationship of the double to its symbolic form is particularly vivid in those prose poems whose narrative movement draws attention to character and situation'.[26]

While Nanda Kaul is full of contradictions, Raka is completely devoid of them. Unlike Nanda Kaul, who discovers her life as a lie (p. 145) in the end, Raka has no compunctions. Nanda Kaul feels she is independent at Carignano, but gradually becomes emotionally dependent on Raka.

> "But now Nanda Kaul seemed unwilling to stop talking, to let Raka out of her sight. There she flopped on her chair a small fish gasping for its native air but the old lady had her on the hook — a sharp bright hook — and held the string tight." (pp. 94-95)

Raka's presence is instrumental in bringing about the spiritual awakening in Nanda Kaul. Prior to her confessing being a liar, and her life a lie, she is filled with concern for everyone and everything around her.

> ...."She well and strong and upright, she ought to protect her. She ought to fight some of the battles." (p. 133)

By rejecting others, Nanda Kaul was rejecting herself. The recognition of her need for Raka, brings about the spiritual awareness which lends her the calm and serenity she was seeking all her life. Her protectiveness for the insect reveals it.

> "Then becoming aware of Nanda Kaul's opaline presence, it lifted itself up on to its hind legs, as if in self-defence, and raised its tiny hands together under its chin, turning its solemn head from side to side as it studied her with exactly the same serene curiosity that marked her face. She put out her ringed hand and gave the lily a little shake, so that the creature tumbled off into the leaves. There it would be safe from birds." (p. 134)

The encounters of Nanda Kaul with Raka and Ila Das not only determine the movement of the novel, but form the symbolic self-portrait of her ideal self. The recognition of her need for others, the craving for love and belongingness, is the fire of the spirit which purges her and forces the confession out of her.

Another journey into the innermost recesses of human psyche is the novel, *Where Shall We Go This Summer.*[27]

Unmistakably ironic in tone, the novel is based on the experiences of Sita, the symbolic hero, whose poetic vision distorts the world of a housewife into a mad pursuit.

'I think, "she said, going back to the suit case and the filling of it," what I'm doing is trying to escape from the madness here, escape to a place where it might be possible to be sane again.'

After twenty years, Sita visits the island, in which her father was a magic figure, because she still believes that the place could work miracles.

> "Ah! oh, now I understand! — it seemed steadily more strange, mistaken. Yet, she had arrived, she was on the island in order to achieve the miracle of not giving birth, wasn't this Manori the island of miracles?"
>
> (*Where Shall We Go This Summer*, p. 31)

Similar to the other novels of Anita Desai, the protagonist is in quest of a meaningful existence; the basic question which seeks an answer sooner or later in every life, to feel one with the universal self. A series of encounters and sense perceptions, help her solve this mystery.

Sita is a passive instrument of portraying this magic of spiritual awareness, which lays bare the infinite reality, hidden to ordinary glance.

Skilful correlation of past and present experiences, determines the poetic design of the novel. When the novel begins, Moses, the old servant is waiting for Sita, the present owner of the house and the daughter of the magician father. Sita's father had come to the island to realize his own private vision. The purpose of Sita's visit to the island was also the same, but with a difference. While her father encompassed the whole village, and many outsiders, Sita was an isolated figure, even alienated from her own children.

Contrasts have been drawn between the lives of the father and daughter, between the waiting of Moses, and the waiting of Sita, the search for truth by the father, and the quest of Sita, the impact of father's life and the quiet withdrawal of Sita from the island.

> *Waiting* is the keyword of the novel. The novel begins with it. "Moses *waited*, *waiting* was what he did most of his time." (p. 7)

Sita also waited.

> "Are you waiting for someone? She was occasionally asked by one of three children dashing past or by her husband, as she sat out on the balcony.... I am waiting, she agreed although for what, she could not tell for the two halve's of this grey egg world to fall apart and burst into festival fire-works, a woman's seaweed hair or blood stained feathers?" (p. 54)

Moses' *waiting* is a hypocritical counterpoint to the sincere *waiting* of Sita. Sita's waiting is equivalent to the lyrical poet's cry, who expresses doubt about his search before finding the solution to it.

Sita's faith in the miracle island, and her innuendoes (p. 99) at her father, give rise to a divided point of view. The threads of this divided thinking run parallel, till by the visit of Phoolmaya to Sita (p. 105) they start bending towards each other to make a strand. Sita feels more relaxed although not yet prepared to go back to Bombay. The lines by D.H. Lawrence haunt her.

"Even the slumbrous egg as it labours
under the shell
Patiently to divide and subdivide." (p. 57)

The line between the creative and the destructive had grown thin, hazy and undefinable for Sita (p. 56), that it was not easy for her to merge into her father's magic all of a sudden. To objectify her innermost feelings and sensations, her perceptions have been changed into scenes.

Sita's irrepressible desire to support life and the ravaging forces operating all around her, have been portrayed objectively through the black drama in the crow theatre (p. 38). Her spiritual experience is reflected in the form of the jelly-fish, which serves as the catalyst.

> 'Tossed up and thrown on to the sand bar by the discarding waves, it now lay quite still again as it had inside the skull of that mostly passive and unadventurous sea creature. For Sita's eyes to regard till a sudden pulsing movement inside her reminded of the foetus stranded between her hips and she was startled by the similarity of what floated inside her, mindless and helpless, to this poor washed thing thrown on the beach, opaque and wet and sad.' (p. 124)

Sita not only compares the foetus with the jelly-fish but her ownself also.

> "Perhaps I am only like the jelly-fish washed up by the waves stranded there on the sand bar. I was just stranded here by the sea that's all." (p. 149)

The last image scene in which Sita tries to place her feet in the footprints of her husband, as a kind of game to make walking back easier, (p. 150) brings about recognition unconsciously. She remembers the entire poem and with it all her doubts are dispelled.

The process of creation is both concealed and revealed. The seed in order to grow into a plant has to remain hidden. Sita was engaged in the creative process with the foetus hidden inside her. Her father too was engaged in the creative process, as the island still attested to his magic, but he had his moments of concealment too. Both supported life in their own way. Sita's husband was also engaged in supporting life, by supporting the family. He was also contributing to the creative process substantially although quite unconsciously, unlike Sita who had made such an issue of it. And therefore Sita calls this discovery his triumph.

> 'She knew. She allowed him, then, to have his triumph, not to try to cap it with her verse. He deserved that triumph, purely by being so, unconscious of it, so oblivious.' (p. 151)

The primary personal sensation is converted to the recognition of non-personal values by the lyrical process. Through the symbolic awareness of Sita the author realises her poetic vision.

In the novels discussed above, a uniform structural pattern is visible with marked features of a modern psychological novel. Regarding the novels of Anita Desai, Meena Belliappa observes, "What is new in Anita Desai is the effort to delineate a sensitivity to locale, as it operates within the consciousness of her characters".[28] The nature of the central character is crucial to a fictional technique which places the centre of the novel within a single consciousness. The perceiver whose thoughts and feelings constitute the story, is also the instrument for registering the values of the objective world."[29]

The traits of a modern hero suggested by Irwing Howe,[30] can also be easily traced in the protagonists of Anita Desai.

A fictional character may not fulfil all or many of the traits listed below :

* The modern hero is a man who believes in the necessity of action, yet the moral compulsions that lead him to believe in action, also render him unfit for action (*e.g.*, Nirode, Sita, Nanda Kaul).
* He finds it difficult to reconcile the needs of action with those of being, he must learn that to summon courage he will have to abandon bravery (*e.g.*, Maya, Nirode, Monisha, Nanda Kaul, Sita).
* He knows that he can act with full powers only if he commands for his followers and himself, an implicit belief in the meaningfulness of the human scheme. But the more he commits himself to the gestures of heroism, the more he is persuaded of the absurdity of existence. Gods do not speak to him, prophets do not buoy him,

nor doctrines assuage him (*e.g.*, Nanda Kaul, Maya, Monisha, Sita).

* The modern hero often begins with the expectation of changing the world, but after a time his central question becomes, 'Can I change myself'? (*e.g.*, Sita, Nanda Kaul, Amla, Nirode).
* If the modern hero decides that the world is beyond changing, he may try to create a hermetic world of his own, in which an unhappy few live by a self-willed code that makes possible — they tell themselves — struggle, renewal, and honourable defeat. (Nanda Kaul, Nirode, Sita and Maya)
* Still the modern hero believes in the quest and sometimes in the grail too; only he is no longer persuaded that a quest is necessarily undertaken through public action, and he is unsure as to where the grail can be found. (Maya, Nanda Kaul, Sita, Nirode, Monisha, Amla).
* The modern hero moves from the heroic deed to the heroism of consciousness, a heroism often available in defeat. He comes as a conqueror and stays as a pilgrim. And in consciousness he seeks those moral ends which the hero is traditionally said to have found through the deed.
* The modern hero discovers he cannot be a hero. Yet only through his readiness to face the consequences of this discovery, can he salvage a portion of the heroic. (*e.g.*, almost all the protagonists in the novels of Anita Desai).

Allen Warren Friedman considers the modern novels, "multivalent". He says,

> 'Multivalence is a double edged term : it applies equally to multiple ways of viewing and to multiple ways of being seen. It affords a full spectrum of narrative perspectives. Each perspective is self-conscious and inadequate, but a still possible way of envisaging a reality that remains in flux even while one seeks to perceive and define it.'[31]

In the novels discussed here the protagonists are beset with questions of existence and try to find answers to them in their own way, only to discover that "the true question, the one alone worth asking, cannot and need not be answered, it need only be asked over and over again, forever in new ways".[32]

The novels gain in unity and meaning by including continuous sequences, scenes and images of varying lengths. Desai has successfully retained consecutiveness by engaging the reader at disconnected points, *e.g.*, in *Voices in the City*, after the section on Nirode, Monisha takes over, but begins with an account of Nirode intermingled with her own experiences. Simultaneity is also added to the narration by characters who create events by exposing themselves gradually, for *e.g.*, Arjun's letter in *Cry the Peacock.* In these novels, "The linear is never lost. We are carried into the future as well because we follow not only the actions of the past, but also the mind of the protagonist narrator as it seeks to recapture and depict, and therefore to create the past in the image of the present."[33]

Anita Desai has also retained the logic of unforeseen connections, by forming images and image scenes, which do not cross the boundaries of analogy or credibility and hence are acceptable to the reader.

The process of externalising the subtle experiences of human soul, or the conversations of the mind, require both ingenuity and personal integrity from the writer. Maya's justification of murder, evoking sympathetic response on Monisha's suicide, Amla's affair with Dharma, Sita's sudden awakening to the facts of creation, and Nanda Kaul's confession, are all a result of exquisite artistry and audacious sincerity, and can only be the work of someone for whom art and reality, beauty and truth are one and inseparable. To sum up with the words of Henry James,

> "Experience is never limited and it is never complete; it is an immense sensibility, a kind of huge spider web of the finest silken threads suspended in the chamber of consciousness and catching every airborne particle in its tissue. It is the very atmosphere of the mind, and when the mind is imaginative — much more when it happens to be that of a man of genius — it takes to itself the

faintest hints of life, it converts the very pulses of the air into revelations."[34]

REFERENCES

1. Rene Welleck and Austin Warren, *Theory of Literature* (London : Penguin, 1973), p. 1140.
2. Ralph Freedman, *The Lyrical Novel* (Princeton : University Press, 1973), p. 40.
3. Irwing Howe, "The Idea of the Modern" in *The Idea of the Modern in Literature and Arts*, ed., Irwing Howe (New York : Horizon Press, 1967), pp. 12-13.
4. Meena Belliappa, *Anita Desai, A study of her Fiction* (Calcutta : Writer's Workshop, 1977), p. 52.
5. Meena Belliappa, p. 1.
6. Ralph Freedman, p. 9.
7. Henry James, "*The Art of Fiction*" in Selected Literary Criticism Henry James, ed. Morris Shapira (New York : McGraw Hill, 1965), p. 63.
8. *Ibid.*, p. 57.
9. Ralph Freedman, p. 1.
10. Atma Ram, "An interview with Anita Desai", World Literature written in English, Vol. 16, No. 1, April 1977, p. 101.
11. Anita Desai, "Statement", in *Contemporary Novel*, ed. James Vinson (London : St. James Press, 1972), p. 348.
12. Anita Desai, "Replies to the Questionnaire", *Kakatiya Journal of English Studies*, Vol. 3, No. 1, 1978, p. 4.
13. Irwing Howe, p. 21.
14. Ralph Freedman, pp. 1-38.
15. Anita Desai, "Indian Writer's Problems" in *Perspectives on Anita Desai*, ed. R.K. Shrivastava (Ghaziabad : Vimal Prakashan, 1984), pp. 3-4.
16. Roger Fowler, *Linguistic Criticism* (New York : Oxford University Press, 1986), p. 135.
17. *Ibid.*, p. 138.
18. Anita Desai, *Cry the Peacock* (Delhi : Vision Books, 1983).
19. Ralph Freedman, p. 20.
20. *Ibid.*, p. 21.
21. *Ibid.*, p. 35.
22. Anita Desai, *Voices in the City* (New Delhi : Orient Paperbacks, 1965).
23. Quoted from, Ralph Freedman, *The Lyrical Novel*, p. 20.
24. *Ibid.*, p. 8.
25. Anita Desai, *Fire on the Mountain* (Middlesex : Penguin Books, 1977).

26. Ralph Freedman, p. 32.
27. Anita Desai, *Where Shall We Go This Summer*? (Delhi : Orient Paperbacks, 1975).
28. Meena Belliappa, p. 27.
29. *Ibid*., p. 7.
30. Irwing Howe, pp. 35-36.
31. Allan Warren Friedman, "The Modern Multivalent Novel", in *The Theory of the Novel,* ed. John Halperin (New York : Oxford University Press, 1974), pp. 123-24.
32. Irwing Howe, p. 18.
33. Allan Warren Friedman, p. 133.
34. Henry James, "The Art of Fiction", in *Selected Literary Criticism Henry James*, ed. Morris Shapira (New York : McGraw Hill, 1965), p. 56.

4

RHETORIC OF THE NOVELS OF ANITA DESAI

Rhetoric in ordinary language can be seen as a set of principles or guidelines for getting things done by means of language.

According to Leech & Short, 'Pragmatics and rhetoric are ways in which users implement the cognitive or ideational code of language.'[1]

Wayne Booth considers rhetoric as the 'technique of non-didactic fiction-viewed as the art of communicating with readers'.[2]

David Lodge states that rhetoric is the vehicle of an argument.[3]

Form and idea are inseparable in any literary writing and as Henry James puts it in his essay the 'Art of Fiction' : 'questions of art are questions (in the widest sense) of execution'.[4]

The following aspects of technique need special consideration :

(i) Fictional sequencing.

(ii) Discourse and Discourse situation.

(iii) Types of narration, the narrative voice and tone.

(iv) Speech and thought presentation.

(v) Point of view.

Fictional Sequencing

It is the aspect of presentation of information in a novel. It can be chronological, psychological, or presentational. While the first two are self-explanatory, the third *i.e.*, presentational sequencing requires some explanation. As Leech and Short describe it, the best order of presentation, if one wants to facilitate the reader's processing of information both in fiction writing and in general expository writing is to go from elements which presuppose the least prior knowledge to those which presuppose the most. In presentational sequencing as well as in the other aspects of sequencing the authors artistic sense often shows in the way information is withheld, rather than in the way it is revealed.[5]

All eight novels of Anita Desai have their own individual sequencing.

Beginning with *Cry the Peacock*, in this novel the sequencing is more psychological and presentational than chronological. The first part of the novel describes an event which reveals the inherent qualities of the protagonists and yet the reader is not told anything about their identities. In other words, the death of a pet is all that the novel reveals in the beginning at a point of least supposition, and ends on a point where the reader feels that he knows all about Maya and Gautam, and hence he is not shocked by the end. The interior monologue, the conversation between Maya and Gautam, the hallucinations of Maya, are all detailed psychological analyses of the innermost self of Maya, and though chronologically we feel that time has moved, Desai's deft presentational sequencing patterns it all in flash backs and dramatic modes of soliloquy, giving us the impression of a lifestory.

In *Voices in the City*, presentational sequencing is paramount. The book has been divided into four parts, 'Nirode', 'Monisha', 'Amla' and 'The Mother'. On retrospect, one gets the impression of four different portraits, wrought with great detail but fixed in their places. In fact the presentational sequencing impresses the reader as a study of four lives interlinked and yet compartmentalized in their own way. The psychological awareness is also patterned to reveal the individualities of the three protagonists. The novel does begin promising much but the end is rather abrupt and unconvincing. Amla has had her moment of vision and Monisha is effaced from the scene. Nirode's acceptance of their mother as *Kali* lacks conviction for the reader.

Psychological sequencing in this novel is best traced in the sections dealing with Monisha and Amla. Monisha's journey from self-effacement to self-immolation and Amla's affair with Dharma, captures the impalpable experience of falling in and out of love in very convincing terms. Nirode's personal search surfacing again in the last part of the story does not achieve an intense illusion of reality, including the mental and moral complexities. Prof. Darshan Singh Maini observes, '*Voices in the City* shows a different if less intense Anita Desai'.[6]

Bye-Bye Black Bird is based on chronological sequencing. It is a story of Dev, Adit and Sarah. The novel is divided into three parts. The first part deals with the first impressions of Dev about England, the second titled 'Discovery' and 'Recognition', describes the transition of moods in both Dev and Adit. The last part titled 'Departure' narrates the execution of final decision of Adit and Sarah to leave for India.

The causal chain on which this chronological sequencing is based, somewhere leaves a sense of incompletion. As Booth says, "All good works surprise us and they surprise us largely by bringing to our attention convincing cause and effect patterns which were earlier played down.[7] The decisions of both Dev and Adit are too sudden and contrary to the values professed in the earlier part of the novel and hence create an impression of superficiality, resulting in a lack of sympathy from the reader.

There is little presentational manipulation in the novel, except for the choice of scenes and events for the purpose of foregrounding the theme.

Based on chronological sequencing *A Village by the Sea* reminds one of Mulk Raj Anand's *Coolie*. This novel depicts a social reality in impersonal and explicit terms.

Where Shall We Go This Summer? is again based on psychological and presentational sequencing. Part I Monsoon '67 is followed by Part II Winter '47 and Part III again brings the reader back to Monsoon '67. The past is inseparably embedded in the present. Sita's quest for meaning in life is traced through her thoughts which emanate from her consciousness as a result of past and present experiences.

Fire on the Mountain, follows the pattern of *Where Shall We Go This Summer*. The book is divided into three parts, 'Nanda Kaul at Carignano', 'Raka comes to Carignano', and 'Ila Das leaves Carignano'. The very first sentence of the novel suggests the ironic juxtaposition on which the novel is framed. Nanda Kaul's present and past interwoven into a pattern of image scenes result in a consummate presentational and psychological sequencing. In this novel the end like the beginning is effective and satisfying to the reader's urge for completion.

Clear Light of Day is divided into four parts. Although the chronology of the family has been traced, the sequencing is more in keeping with the psychological and presentational order. The commentary is direct and impersonal but the writer selects and highlights events and episodes to create a necessary background for the moment of 'recognition' in the life of Bim, to justify the ethical stance of the novel. The beginning gives a general impression of the family but withholds details for dramatic presentation in the middle of the novel. The forgiveness and surge of emotions towards the end seem natural and acceptable as Bim is forced into introspection and self-analysis by Tara's visit.

In Custody, the last novel included here, follows chronological sequencing and is interspersed with internal and external perspectives. The causal chain is unbroken till the end. However the technique of 'Free Indirect Discourse', makes the writing full of subjective element.

Discourse and Discourse Situation

'Discourse means linguistic communication' seen as transaction between speaker and hearer, in prose fiction it is the author and the reader.[8]

Discourse in prose fiction also has an extended meaning of rapport between the writer and the reader.

> "Every writer assumes that he shares a common fund of knowledge and experience with his readers. This general background not only consists of common facts but also knowledge of historical events, literary works and even quotations from the latter. Because the author can assume knowledge which any particular reader might not necessarily have, we have to conclude that the addressee in literary communication is not the reader, but what may be more conveniently termed as the implied reader, a hypothetical personage who shares with the author not just background knowledge but also a set of

> presuppositions, sympathies and standards of what is pleasant and unpleasant, good and bad, right and wrong."[9]

In keeping with the term implied reader, Booth has used the term 'implied author'.

> "It is a curious fact that we have no terms either for this created second self or for our relationship with him. None of our terms for various aspects of the narrator is quite accurate. 'Persona', 'mask' and 'narrator' are sometimes used but they more commonly refer to the speaker in the work who is after all only one of the elements created by the implied author and who may be separated from him by large ironies. Narrator is usually taken to mean the 'I' of the work but the 'I' is seldom if ever identical with the implied image of the artist."[10]

In other words the views expressed in a writing cannot be automatically ascribed to the author. The arrangement may be arbitrary according to the needs of artistic arrangement. Booth further adds :

> "Some aspects of the implied author may be inferred through tonal variations, but his major qualities will depend also on hard facts of action and character in the tale that is told. The 'implied' author chooses, consciously or unconsciously what we read, we infer him as an ideal literary created version of the real man; he is the sum of his own choices."[11]

Viewed from this angle, the novels of Anita Desai reveal interesting information about their implied authors.

In the first novel, *Cry the Peacock*, the implied author has a separate identity in Part I and Part III but he is merged with the character of Maya in the II Part of the book, which also happens to be the major portion or the main story. As Prof. Maini says, *Cry the Peacock* is a story rendered through the consciousness of Maya and in her own agonised idiom.'[12] Although in the beginning the description is impersonal and uninvolved, gradually the implied reader is lead to understand her dilemma and by the time the novel reaches its climax the reader is totally wrapped up in her argument. The first person narration, full of rhetorical questions, are direct addresses to the reader, inviting his judgement on events. As a result the reader feels drawn towards Maya.

> 'Why should I love him? I wish I did not! ? But then, what is it there for if not to feel sorrow? There never lived a bird that did not know a storm, a stone, a wound. And I, an adult thinking woman, had no more right to happiness than I had been taught by Gautam, to regard as a privilege.'[13]
>
> (*Cry the Peacock*, pp. 201-2)

The implied author's role is to create the contrasting world of sensitive Maya and practical Gautam. Anita Desai consciously filters information so that towards the end Maya's version seems fully justified and wins the whole-hearted sympathy of the reader, or to use Booth's phrase, the reader is caught in the trap of (Maya's) 'suffering consciousness'. (Booth, p. 383)

In *Voices in the City* the implied author seeks to portray 'the illusion and conflicts that upset modern Indian young people, sensitive, educated and excessively self-conscious, forced by the circumstances of living in Calcutta'.[14]

The implied author is distant from his characters, as well as from the reader, except on the portion titled 'Monisha', where implied author and the character merge. The major part of the novel is written through a third person centre of consciousness. Against the background of Calcutta, the three figures of brothers and sisters stand out helpless and puny, till finally they are merged with the eternal flux of life epitomized in the figures of *Kali* and *Calcutta*. The tacit agreement between the implied author and reader is dubious at this point of sudden religio-cultural conformity in the novel.

In *Bye-Bye Black Bird* the implied author chooses to remain distant from the characters by juxtaposing two individuals faced with the same choice. Both Dev and Adit could either stay in England or come back to their motherland. As R.S. Sharma remarks, 'the blackbird stands both for the temptation and the gloom, that this temptation creates for the ex colonial. If Adit is free of his temptation, Dev is free of his gloom. The novel therefore rightly bids the black bird a "bye-bye".[15] The implied reader is expected to know a lot about England and India and the difference in culture and social values, in order to understand the full significance of the choices made by Dev and Adit.

The implied author is in full control of the narrative in *Clear Light of Day*. From the beginning, it is a third person narration with strong personal markers. But this does not change the stance taken by the implied author. The story of Bim, Tara, Raja and Baba traced through the long years, carries a multiplicity of values. What gains reader's sympathy is 'that all the elements that threaten to disrupt the pattern of life in all its aspects are brought under control through love, understanding, forgiveness and mutual acceptance. The triumph of these values over despair and destruction leaves the reader joyously participating in the musical recital that concludes the novel'.[16]

The implied author and real author are·one in the novel *Fire on the Mountain*. The juxtaposition of three lives in exile for different reasons makes the novel structurally compact and complete. The ironic note on which the novel begins,

> 'the scented sibilance.'
>
> 'This was the chief virtue of Kasauli of course — its starkness.'
>
> 'While Nanda Kaul slit eyed burned on the knoll.'[17]
>
> (*Fire on the Mountain*, pp. 3-5)

evokes sympathetic understanding from the reader because as Booth says 'the most human themes are those that reflect the moral ambiguities of life'.[18]

The narrative distance is consistently maintained till the end and the subjective intentions of the implied author are to a great extent objectively achieved.[19]

The third person, stance of the implied author in, *In Custody*, winds reader's assurance by its acceptance of realistic human condition. The protagonist Deven Sharma, is goaded on to action by the sheer force of his nobility, but is ultimately led to accept defeat with the recognition of his failure in the mission he undertakes, all because of his lack of confidence and tact.

The implied author and the real author are the same. Though the implied author and Deven come very close to each other in the passages where the technique of 'Free Direct thought' and 'Free Indirect thought' have been adopted in narration.

Varying degrees of distance can be marked between the implied author and the main character in the novel *Where Shall We Go This Summer*. The story is mostly a depiction of the consciousness of Sita, but being a third person narration, the implied author intrudes in the guise of minor characters in the novel. However the authenticity of the narrative is not diminished as 'degrees of psychic and physical vividness are created'.[20]

A Village by the Sea conforms to the traditional methods of omniscient author approach. The implied author depicts rural as well as urban life successfully. Moreover the author captures the spirit of the two different ways of life and presents a combination in the character of Hari. The reader is thus drawn to accept the social change which is slowly but surely taking place in India.

Types of Narration, the Narrative Voice and Tone

Critics have for a long time distinguished between author and the narrator. It is also noticed that the narrator does not always address the reader but may address person or persons in the novel itself.

Two types of narration however are quite common. 'I' narration, or the 'first person narration' is the technique adopted by epistolatory fiction writers, and novels with first person account of one's own or someone else's life experiences.

As Leech and Short put it, 'the choice of a first person narrator where the 'I' is also a primary character in the story, produces a personal relationship with the reader which inevitably tends to bias the reader in favour of the narrator/character'.[21]

Wayne Booth remarks that the personal account of 'I' narration makes the narration dramatic, intense and lively.[22]

'First person narration gives perspective, variety and authenticity to the narrative.'[23]

Trollope, however, observes the perils of first person narrative. He writes, "It is always dangerous to write from the point of 'I'. The reader is unconsciously taught to feel that the writer is glorifying himself, and rebels against the self-praise. Or otherwise the 'I' is pretentiously humble, and offends from exactly the other point of view".[24]

Henry James in his preface to the Ambassadors thinks that the first person (narration) in the long piece, is a form foredoomed to looseness.[25]

In modern fiction extensive use is made of first person narration. "The 'I' becomes a de-personalised expression of the suffering modern sensibility. In order to control the fluidity of their more exuberant egotism, a story within a story device is used allowing the 'I' self-expression but confining it within the framework of an outer third person narration".[26]

'Third person narration', is based on impersonal style of narration. The presentation is direct. The implied author and narrator are merged. The implied author claims absolute knowledge and hence an omniscient stance is adopted. This method allows the writer a large scope for depiction of objective as well as subjective states, and also facilitates the description of social and historical events. However the very omniscience becomes a threat to the economy and architecture of the composition because there are no limits to the freedom of the author.

Booth envisages certain dangers of this kind of writing. He writes, "There can be no intensity of illusion if the author is present, constantly reminding us of his unnatural wisdom. Indeed there can be no illusion of life where there is no bewilderment and the omniscient author is obviously not bewildered. The process most like the process of life is that of observing events through a convincing human mind not a god-like mind unattached to the human condition".[27]

Another kind of narration advocated by Henry James is the 'indirect and oblique view'.[28] This method of story writing gives an account of strictly selective impressions; from omniscient narrative by concentrating on the inner reactions to a given situation of a restricted member of characters (sometimes indeed, confining itself exclusively to a single viewpoint); and from the 'stream of consciousness', by being less interested in the processes of ordinary undisciplined human consciousness than in illustrating the workings of this consciousness when it is directed to a particular end.[29]

In modern fiction, the indirect mode of narration is considered superior to any other mode. In this method the author renounces the privilege of direct intervention and allows his characters to mould themselves. Such authors agree with Percy Lubbock[30] that the art of fiction does not begin until the novelist thinks of history as a matter to be shown to be so exhibited that it tells itself.

In the writings of Anita Desai there is a combination of all three types of narration. Desai adopts 'I' narration technique in only two novels, *Cry the Peacock* and *Voices in the City* . *In Cry the Peacock*, Part I and Part III serving as prologue and epilogue, are third person narration. The main drama, Part II is narrated by Maya, the primary character of the novel, who traces her own psychic developments from normal longing for love and life to obsessive tendencies with death and destruction.

In, *Voices in the City*, the section on 'Monisha' is written in the first person, presented as pages from her diary. It is true that both these accounts tend to gain the reader's sympathy and lend an air of intensity to the description. Self-revealing as the writings are, the account nowhere degenerates into egotism or falsehood but attracts our attention and gains reader's confidence, as the candid confessions of both the characters are unmistakably the very cry of the soul, the sanctity of which only calls for reverence. Anita Desai's, *A Village by the Sea*, is an example of direct telling in which the omniscient author does not explicitly interfere with the subjective world of the characters.

In the remaining writings, Anita Desai follows the Jamesian way 'of standing above the story and taking a broad view of many things, of transcending the limits of immediate scene'.[31] Through the third person stance, Anita Desai is able to evoke a strong feeling of closeness with the characters. This effect is achieved through the device of 'Free Indirect Discourse', applied extensively throughout her works. It is because of this device, the constant presence of the author is not felt, disturbing us with forced commentary

Narrative Voice and Tone

Other important features of rhetoric of fiction are the narrative voice and the tone adopted by the author.

Authors and narrators are not synonymous in prose fiction. Fowler has apty described,

> "Whereas plays traditionally consist wholly of dialogue, other literary forms such as novels and short stories mix dialogue with monologic narrative and commentary. At first glance there might appear to be a very sharp distinction between passages of dialogue where the character's voices seem to take the stage, and passages of prose writing where the narrator takes charge. But in fact narrative discourse engages in another class of dialogic interactions between the narrator and the reader. By dialogic here I do not refer to text which has the superficial structure of dialogue *i.e.*, language which is set out as different 'speeches' attributed to different speakers rather this is an implicit dialogue where the language implies an interaction of views or values, or more overtly the presence of an attentive and thinking 'narratee'. There are a number of techniques, by which the narrating voices' engagement with these narrated voices can be signified."[32]

In simpler terms we may say that the different forms adopted by the authors voices may be termed as the narrative voice. In direct, personal narration location of narrative voice is easier, but in impersonal narration careful analysis of addresser and addressee relationship is required for correct inferences where direct commentary is not employed on a character, the authorial views can be indicated less directly through infiltrations into the character's speech itself for *e.g.*, when Ila Das rings up Nanda Kaul the words she stresses in her speech give out her feelings for Nanda Kaul.

'We have not met *for ages, dear.*'
'But Nanda, how *marvellous,*'
'Your *great-grand-daughter* did you say?'

(*Fire on the Mountain*, p. 21)

Sometimes the writer creates a narrating voice juxtaposing authorial views with those ascribed to his presumed readers or narratees. For *e.g.*, The magic of Sita's father still prevails in the Island of Manori, twenty years after his death. Sita doubts the sincerity of her father, but the islanders still remember him as a wonder working person. The author reiterates this point in the end of the novel through the dialogues of village people. Juxtaposing these authorial views Sita says,

> "What was its composition? she wondered. What were its elements? Partly, she felt, it had been his appearance — so trivial, so insignificant a part of a man, as one likes to believe yet it had played its part. He had been ugly, grotesquely ugly, so as to arouse first notice, then pity, finally regard — a hypnotized kind of notice and regard."[33]

Representing authorial views, the villagers pass their verdict on Sita :

> Her husband suddenly sang out in a quaver. "He was like a god — a magic man."
>
> "Magic", agreed Jamila rolling her tongue inside her mouth.
>
> "He did magic".
>
> "Who can forget" Moses suddenly thundered, scowling at his audience of two.
>
> "No one, no one" the sick man cooed, calming him.
>
> "But *she* — ". Jamila spat.
>
> "She was plain. Not like him. Too plain, Moses."
>
> "Mad too," he contemptuously growled.

Thus location of narrative voice at different levels of discourse is important for understanding the communicative functions of a text. The change in narrative voice may be at different levels of discourse, and the collapsing of levels is very common in the novel. For *e.g.*, Sita who doubted her father's sincerity in the end calls herself an actress a pretender.

> "His biographies and his critics...made them hold their tongues. Practical achievements and shady hocus-pocus wound in and out of each other to form one inextricable strand, knotted but whole."
>
> (*Where Shall We Go This Summer*, p. 74)
>
> "She felt tired, dishevelled and vacant as she was — like a player at the end of the performance...she had actually been playing the part here of an actress in a theatrical performance and was now to return to a life of retirement, off-stage." (p. 74)

As Leech and Short put it, "novels as discourses have highly individual architectures. This is especially so when we address different interlocutors at different points in his story."[34]

Interesting indeed are the mirror views of modern fiction which portray the inner conflicts of a character, separating him into more than one entity and thus create more than one narrative voice out of a single character. An interesting example is Desai's mirror view from *Cry the Peacock.*

> 'And while I held my soul, still burning in my hands, I saw my body detach itself from it and float away, to rest upon the dim mirror where I could gaze upon it from a cool distance. I studied it, absorbed; the round, childish face, pretty, plump and pampered, its smooth, silken skin with one, small velvet mole; the small, shell like ears curling around petty ignorance; the soft overall lips arched with vulnerable sweetness.... (*Maya's physical self*). But it was not a face that a man like Gautam could love. He might be charmed by it, momentarily, diverted by it for a while but to capture him entirely, if a fleshy face could do it 'it' would have to be a finer one...bereft of the weakness of impulses, aloof from coarseness and freshness. (*Maya's intellectual self*) and I gazed long at each feature of the image before me, so like a painting on a chocolate box and hated it fiercely. Hate was a new emotion to me, and in trespassing upon it, I entered a new vista of knowledge. I forced myself into believing that I could see now what must be the reason for my hating it so, for Gautam's spurning it — visible to our subconscious only. (*Maya's subconscious self*)
>
> (*Cry the Peacock*, pp. 105-6)

The shift in the three levels of discourse is easily discernable.

Authorial tone and narrative voice are closely linked. 'Tone means the stance or attitude taken by an implied author towards his readers and towards (part of) his message'.[35] It is assumed that there is a symmetry between the attitudes the author expresses and the attitude elicited from the reader. This symmetry is based on the notion of *distance* and in fact this symmetry is never complete as the literary interests which merge the reader and the writer, can rarely be combined to perfection in a novel.

Wayne Booth[36] has classified the interests or values which interest a reader and thus are available for technical manipulation in fiction.

(1) *Intellectual or cognitive* — a reader has a strong intellectual curiosity about facts, the true interpretation, the true reasons, the true origins, the true motives, or the truth about life itself.

(2) *Qualitative or aesthetic* — The reader has a strong desire to see any pattern or form completed, or to experience a further development of qualities of any kind.

(3) *Practical* — The reader has or can be made to have a strong desire for the success or failure of characters he loves or hates, admires or detests, or he can be made to hope or fear a change in the quality of a character.

Booth[37] has also classified the various distances between the author, characters of the novel and the reader. He writes :

> "In any reading experience there is an implied dialogue among author, narrator, the other characters and the reader. Each of the four can range in relation to each other from identification to complete opposition on any axis of value-moral, intellectual, aesthetic and even physical."

(1) The narrator may be more or less distant from the implied author. The distance may be moral. It may be intellectual. It may be physical or temporal.

(2) The narrator may be more or less distant from the characters in the story he tells. He may differ morally, intellectually or temporally.

(3) The narrator may be more or less distant from the reader's own norms for example, physically, emotionally, morally.

(4) The implied author may be more or less distant from the reader. The distance may be intellectual, aesthetic or moral.

(5) The implied author (carrying the reader with him)

may be more or less distant from the other characters. Again the distance can be on any axis of value.

The relation between author and subject matter is also one of variable distance, depending on the implied author's knowledge, sympathy and values of the implied authors, and those of characters and society, which he portrays.

Leech and Short[38] have observed certain stylistic ingredients which determine authorial tone. They are evaluative terms and evaluative inferences, ironic contrast and reversal, direct appeal to the reader through rhetorical questions and the like, indirect appeals to the reader through generic statements and other references to a commonality of experience and judgement. All these lead to a complex weighing up of one attitude against another, especially of sympathetic identification against ironic distance. The authorial tone is subtle, complex and variable in a way which gives solidity to the presence of the implied author.

Authorial tone, like authorial point of view, therefore takes on a multiplicity of values. The irony is only one point in a spectrum of tone, which can extend in theory from pure compassion to pure denunciation, but in practice contains some measure, however slight of both.

Irony can register varying degrees of distance or severity, hanging from a satirical bitterness to a benevolent awareness of the contradictory impulses.

In Anita Desai we have two outstanding examples of this. *Fire on the Mountain*, begins with a satirical bitterness, but in the end the authorial tone is softened and full of understanding for the primary character Nanda Kaul. In *Where Shall We Go This Summer*, the author reveals a benevolent awareness of the contradictory impulses which upset Sita, but towards the end she overcomes the disintegrating forces and regains her authentic self.

"Give me the right word and the right accent", wrote Joseph Conrad in his 'Familiar Preface' "and I will move the world".[39]

Tone then is a manifestation of author's feelings for events and situations and is directly connected with the beliefs of the author.

"In truth every novelist must begin by creating for himself a world, great or little, in which he can honestly believe", says Conrad.[40] If an author is not quite honest or if he is lacking in courage his creation will lack the conviction necessary to gain the reader's faith in his apprehension of reality. It is the ring of sincerity in an author's tone which captivates the reader.

Belief or sincerity does not mean discovery of truth through imitation of life but as Walter F. Wright in his essay 'Tone in Fiction', suggests :

> 'What great fiction does is to suggest an attitude towards the multiform and varicoloured incidents and phenomena of which we are or can become aware. Its validity in reference to truth is not the truth it presents, but in the perspective it suggests.... A great work of fiction does ask the reader to see "through" the author's eyes and above all to feel.... For through complete submission to the tone which the novelist has created the reader experiences an imaginative refreshment, perhaps even a rebirth when he turns from the novel back to his sole self, the circumstances which surround him are no more ordinary than before. But he is inclined to feel them in a new way. It is this, which in the Jamesian sense, represents the madness — and the miracle — of art.'[41]

The distinguished role of narrative voices and the resultant tone in the novels of Anita Desai make an interesting study.

In *Cry the Peacock*, the two separate voices of Maya and Gautam determine the tone. The novel begins and ends with a third voice which may be termed neutral, but the major writing registers two distinct voices supporting arguments in two different directions. While Maya's voice gains in strength as the novel progresses, Gautam's becomes feebler and feebler, till in the end we hear the triumphant call of Maya after she accomplishes the deed. The voices of minor characters serve as contrast to the dominant voice of Maya, resulting in added justification of her line of thinking.

The feeling evoked by the novel is not univalent but multivalent. The reader is left with a sense of ambiguity. There is a clash between intellectual and aesthetic interests. Even though the reader sympathises with Maya, her final act of impulse is not justifiable to a sane mind. Aesthetically, the minute recordings of Maya's sub-conscious and its description in palpable terms is a marvel by itself. The reader is captivated by the beauty of the vivid picture and yet at the same time he does not stop sympathizing with Gautam altogether. As a result the feelings evoked are ambiguous.

Voices in the City, as the title suggests is a concourse of voices not necessarily concordant. Foregrounded against the din of Calcutta city, the major characters have their own conflicts to settle through their prominent vocalizations, but the author's voice is deliberate and clear, editing, commenting and marshalling events. An earnest effort to grasp the meaning of life determines the tone of the novel.

While Nirode is trying to seek an identity through his transactions with different people, young and old, Monisha and Amla in their restricted world are also trying to solve the mystery of life. This direct probe into the fundamental concerns of life makes it a novel based on intellectual interests. The aesthetic interest is best catered for in the account of Monisha and Amla. Both of them gain reader's sympathy.

The prevailing seriousness of tone is accompanied by intense dramatic irony, evident from the beginning of the novel.

> 'On the platform people loitered in various attitudes of nervousness impatience and regret.'
>
> 'So it seemed to the red-shirted coolies', etc.[42]

This free play of irony can also be marked in the description of minor characters, the generic observations on Bengali women, the typical family life of middle class Bengalis, (Jiban's family), the love and vanity of past grandeur (Sonny and Sonny's family). The remarks of Nirode on present day society are all full of satirical bitterness.

On the other hand the candid expression of Monisha, Amla and Dharma's feelings fills the reader with a sense of awe and acceptance for the unavoidable springs of nature in man.

In the last part of the novel, there is a sudden collapsing of levels of discourse. The finality of tone with which the 'mother' is described as *Kali* is something the reader is not prepared for. Awareness of sudden truth like sudden change is shocking. The novel ends thus diminishing the effect it had created from Part I to Part III.

Bye-Bye Black Bird has two prominent narrative voices *i.e.*, of Dev and Adit. The third voice is that of Sarah who seems to be the catalyst exerting a strong influence on both Dev and Adit. The narrator adopts the tone of an amused observer, witnessing this drama of black birds. The matter of fact tone continues throughout the novel. The author neither condemns nor acclaims the decision of the two friends. The novel ends on a note of compromise, Dev content with his new home in England, and the Sen's already on their way to India.

Clear Light of Day has the balanced force of two narrative voices, the implied author and Bim. It is Bim's consciousness that the novel projects. The implied author discloses the layers of her consciousness formed over the years, through the characters of Tara and Raja. Tara's voice although subdued is a constant reminder to Bim to strike a happy balance in life, while Raja's unseen presence is responsible for the turmoil in Bim's soul and the succeeding calm when Bim is reconciled with him. The novel caters to the practical interests of the reader because he is already sympathetic towards Bim and when in the end she realizes happiness in her own way, the reader has a sense of victory.

The novel in the beginning has an atmosphere of decadence but ends on a note of rejuvenation.

In Custody, is mainly the story of Deven Sharma. The implied author and this character come very close to each other and sometimes merge into each other. The other voices are that of Murad's (Deven's counterpart), and Nur Shahjahanabadi, the Urdu poet, and minor characters, Sarla, Trivedi, Nur's wives etc. Murad and Deven represent two different life styles, and although Deven Sharma is the less successful of two, it is he who gains, the reader's sympathy because of his honesty and uprightness. Even Nur, with all his poetry and fame fails to impress us because of his disordered personal life. Deven, though not prosperous displays a reverence for all that is good and noble in life, and the reader is won over by the sheer power of goodness which may not give us any material reward but is its own reward.

Where Shall We Go This Summer, is marked by the conflicting voices of Sita and her father. The implied author stays in the background. It is only in the beginning and the end that the implied author comments indirectly on the person of Sita through the minor characters in the novel. The implicit dialogue and monologues of Sita form the core of the novel.

The novel has a free play of satire. From open ridicule to innuendoes leading to direct condemnation, the novel is a deft study in analogies and contrasts. The ambiguous tone continues throughout, till towards the end when all doubts are dispelled for Sita.

The novel evokes mixed feelings of sympathy for Sita and doubts about her father's sincerity and *vice versa*. However, this does not dispel our belief in the writer's intentions, as a mature reader knows, how natural it is to misjudge and the satisfaction one gets in humbly acknowledging ones mistakes.

In *Fire on the Mountain*, the author's voice is in direct juxtaposition to that of Nanda Kaul. The author narrates and interprets at the same time. The evaluative terms and inferences, ironic contrast and reversal and rhetorical questions, all very prominent in this writing, highlight the irony of tone. This irony of tone is coupled with irony of fate which mellows Nanda Kaul's personality and allows the reader to penetrate her innerself, which is full of longings for love and companionship.

Authorial voice changes from scene to scene. Raka and Ila Das are described in impersonal tones with complete objectivity, while Nanda Kaul engages the mind of the author. Towards the end, the voices of Nanda Kaul and the author merge in the confession of Nanda Kaul.

The tone of ironic disapproval gradually changes to tacit agreement, and finally to sympathy towards the end. Once the reader is informed about the neglect and rebuff suffered by Nanda Kaul, he no longer considers her a brutal snob but becomes tolerant of her ideology, and in the end he is left with feelings of regret for the irretrievable.

A Village by the Sea, is fully controlled by the authorial voice. A sympathetic tone towards the suffering humanity of Indian villages, prevails. A ray of hope for better days to come marks the end of this writing.

Speech and Thought Presentation

'Monologue and conversation are termed as sub-discourse of the overarching discourse which is novel itself.'[43]

Conversation in a novel consists of dialogue between different characters, or onesided conversation between author and the reader.

According to J.L. Austin and J.R. Searle,[44] "When people utter sentences they also perform acts of various kinds, such as declaring, asking, requesting, commanding, promising, so on. The pragmatic force of an utterance and its semantic sense work together. Semantics is concerned with the representation through the language system of referential reality. Pragmatics is concerned with the enactment through language of situational reality". Austin and Searle[45] also observed that language also has a pragmatic function. Utterances are used to perform actions as well as to communicate propositions true or false. This principle is easy to grasp in connection with certain utterances containing performative verbs such as, promise, declare, name, baptize, request, order, guarantee etc.

Speech acts are the chief mechanism by which conversation is maintained as a practical interaction as well as chanelling of ideas.

Conversational Implicature

The term implicature has been proposed by the philosopher H.P. Grice.[46] An implicature is a proposition emerging from something that is said but not actually stated by the words uttered, nor logically derivable from them. It must therefore be a product of the relationship between utterance and context, and a vital part of context would be the knowledge and motives of speaker and addressee.

Grice suggests that when people converse with one another they acknowledge a kind of tacit agreement to cooperate conversationally towards mutual ends. This agreement he calls the 'Cooperative Principle'. When one abides by the cooperative principle, one agrees to act according to various rules, or rather maxims, as Grice calls them. One must tell the truth and make remarks which are relevant to the conversation. The four maxims are as follows :

(1) *The maxim of quantity* : Give the required amount of information not too much or too little.

(2) *The maxim of quality* : Do not say that for which you lack evidence or which you believe to be false.

(3) *The maxim of relation* : Make your contributions relevant to the purpose in hand.

(4) *The maxim of manner* : Avoid obscurity ambiguity, unnecessary prolixity and be orderly.

These conversational maxims are often violated. These violations may be clandestine or ostentatious. When this happens the listener perceives the difference between what the speaker says and what he means by what he says.

The concepts of 'Speech Acts' and 'Implicature' are important tools in the study of linguistic communication.

As stated earlier, conversation in a novel consists of dialogue between different characters or the onesided conversation between author and the reader. Direct conversation — between author and reader can be marked by the following ingredients. Use of generic present and use of aphoristic present tense, the implicatures drawn from characters' speech by the readers, authorial commentary and the implicature derived out of character speech, unknown to characters themselves.

Different Modes of Speech Presentation

Presence of formal linguistic features and reader's knowledge of extra linguistic contextual factors decide the mode of speech.

In fictional prose there are various ways of speech and thought presentation.

Free Direct Speech (FDS) — The quotation marks and the reporting clause are removed from the speech.

Advantages — The characters speak to the reader more immediately without the intervention of the narrator.

The Narrative Report of Speech Acts (NRSA) — Where only a minimal account of the statement is given.

Example — 'They say all her hair was burnt off, even her eye-lashes, when she went in to save her cat.'

(*Fire on the Mountain*, p. 53)

Advantages — It is useful for summarizing relatively unimportant stretches of conversation.

Free Indirect Speech (FIS). — The speech in which reporting clause is omitted, but where tense and pronoun selection are those associated with indirect speech.

Example — "As the rain softened, her voice rose, unnaturally. He travelled all over Tibet, had the strangest experiences. He spent nights in tiger-infested bamboo forests where the people used to burn green bamboos that would burst at the joints with such loud explosions as to frighten off wild animals for miles."

(*Fire on the Mountain*, p. 84)

Advantages — Although FIS is not a reproduction of original speech, it is more than a mere indirect rendering of the original. Novels written in the narrative present can also have FIS. FIS allows the reader a sense of immediacy and avoids continual repetition of the reporting clause. Used in highlighting and backgrounding of speech according to the role and attitude of characters.

Direct Thought (DT) — Speech with the reporting verbs, thought, mused, pondered, reflected etc.

Free Indirect Thought (FIT) — Like FIS the reporting verbs are absent in FIT. Only an indirect account of thoughts is given.

Example — 'So she leaned upon the gate and watched over her with a kind of fierceness. She, well and strong and upright, she ought to protect her she ought to fight some of her battles.'

(*Fire on the Mountain*, p. 133)

Advantages — It puts us directly inside the character's mind. The reader feels that he is getting a more direct and vivid representation of the characters' thoughts as they happen.

Narrative Report of Thought Acts (NRTA) — Implies the narrator's account of a character's thoughts.

When Nanda Kaul learns about Raka's coming to Carignano, some of her thoughts have been described thus :

> 'Now, to bow again, to let the noose slip once more round her neck that she had thought was freed fully, finally... . Now to converse again when it was silence she wished, to question and follow up and make sure of another's life and comfort and order, to involve oneself; to involve another'.
>
> (*Fire on the Mountain*, p. 19)

To achieve stylistic effects Anita Desai adopts varieties of speech and thought presentations. One can notice different versions of them in a single passage. For *e.g.*, in the following passage the writer has included, Free Indirect Thought, Free Direct Thought, Direct Speech and Free Direct Speech, along with narrative report.

> 'Deven was shocked (Free IT). He looked furtively to the left and the right. They were walking up the stairs to the main hall (Narrative Report). Anyone could have heard even someone on the staff (FDT — Deven's consciousness). His eyebrows crept together in a furry scowl (Narrative Report). 'Please, Murad, leave me now,' he muttered anxiously; (Direct Speech), hunching his shoulders and clutching his books to his chest. (Narrative Report), 'I must go to my class'[47] (Free Direct Speech).
>
> (*In Custody*, p. 10)

Free Indirect Thought and Narrative Report of Thought Acts, dominate the writings of Anita Desai. The psychological nature of her novels makes it a natural choice.

Another passage to illustrate her use of NRTA and FIT.

> But Raka seemed not to enjoy the picture of the caged animals devouring the fish (NRTA). The great grandmother spotted the hurt in the child's eyes (NRTA) and abruptly she put another in its place (NRSA). New as she was to the game (NR) she was becoming an adept, she had a talent she saw (here 'saw' is equivalent to thought) for giving the child a slide-show, coloured and erratic. (FIT), one slide would appear upside down, or there would be a whole series that fluttered past too rapidly to be seen, but now and then appeared steady, glowing and riveting (FIT) and then Nanda Kaul straightened up in pride (NR).
>
> (*Fire on the Mountain*, p. 96)

Desai's variety of speech presentation also includes FIS in first person mode with present tense forms.

Example : 'I put my hands to my mouth, then turn and run back into the house where I know there to be a bowl of ripe fruit gleaming on the polished teakwood of the buffet. Bearing two golden bananas in each hand — more I cannot hold — I come rushing out again, race up to the bear, then stop short, for he is so wonderously large, so powerfully dark, standing there on his hind-legs in an attitude of mourning'.

(*Cry the Peacock*, p. 87)

Some general observations regarding speech and thought presentation in Desai's novels are as follows :

(i) Her writings are marked by a mixture of authorial voice or narrative report, Free Direct thought, Free Indirect thought, Direct speech and Direct thought and Free Indirect speech, alongwith narrative report of speech and thought acts.

(ii) The novelist practices Free Indirect Discourse, which means interweaving of characters' subjective feelings with authors account of the characters inner state. By this method the author juxtaposes two or more sets of values.

(iii) There is more frequent use of Free Indirect thought than Free Indirect speech, the result is, we are directly inside the character's mind.

(iv) Combination of Direct Speech with Free Indirect thought makes the presentation dramatic.

(v) The narrative focus being on the mind of the character, thought presentation techniques often produce soliloquy.

Point of View

'The slanting of the fictional world towards reality as apprehended by a particular participant or set of participants is the fictional point of view.'[48]

The person whose point of view is represented is the reflector of the fiction.

> 'A fiction writer, although not compelled to take one person's point of view, can voluntarily limit, his omniscience to those things which belong to one person's model of reality. He can also vary the fictional point of view, sometimes claiming authorial omniscience, sometimes giving us one character's version of events. Sometimes that of another. He can even take the point of view of an animal, or of a man on the point of death, bypassing the problem of authenticity.'[49]

Fictional point of view, by the standard authorial omniscience can be regarded as a selective withholding of omniscience.

Roger Fowler[50] distinguishes three senses of the phrase, point of view — ideological, psychological and spatio-temporal.

Temporal point of view refers to the impression which a reader gains of events moving rapidly or slowly in a continuous chain or isolated segments. It also includes disruptions of the natural flow of time by, for example, flashbacks, previsions or interweaving of stories which concern different time spheres.

Spatial corresponds to the viewing position in visual arts. Represents objects, people, buildings, landscapes etc. Focus on certain points *i.e.*, the viewing position of the narrator.

Ideological point of view concerns a set of values, a belief system communicated by the language.

A novel may have one ideological system or plural ideological systems. These plural points of view may be in conflicting relationship. A single set of values is not so interesting as opposed to different values in a work. In major novels the underlying values are complex and ironical. Different points of view in distinct and contrasting linguistic styles, constantly challenging and contradicting each other give the novel an argumentative and dynamic structure.

Ideological point of view may be expressed directly or indirectly. In the first case a narrator or a character may directly indicate his or her judgements and beliefs by the use of variety of modal structures. Modality is the grammar of explicit comment, the means by which people express the degree of commitment to the truth of the propositions they utter and their views or desirability or otherwise of the states of affairs referred to. The forms of modal expression include :

Modal Auxiliaries — may, might, must, shall, should, need to, ought to etc. These words signal caution or confidence to various degrees : something might happen, something will happen, must happen.

Modal adverbs or sentence adverbs — Certainly, probably, surely, perhaps etc. Also adjectival versions in such constructions as 'It is certain that... .

Evaluative adjectives and adverbs — Lucky, luckily, fortunately, regrettably, and many others.

Verbs of knowledge, prediction and evaluation : seem, believe, guess, foresee, approve, dislike etc.

Generic sentences — generalized propositions claiming universal truth.

A writer thus may employ the above device to make explicit a character's or his own beliefs and ideas. The writer may also choose to develop a certain ideological point of view as the book progresses.

Psychological or Perceptual Point of View

This concerns the question of who is presented as the observer of the events of a narrative, whether the author or a participating character : and the various kinds of discourse associated with different relationships between author and character. Fowler[51] envisages two kinds of perspectives, internal and external. Internal perspective is further divided into Type A and Type B.

Internal narration, Type 'A' is entirely from the point of view of a character's consciousness. It is subjective in nature and is generally a first person account. If third person narration is followed the writing has strong personal markers and internal monologue.

Internal perspective, Type 'B' — generally takes an omniscient stance. It follows third person narration consistently. There is reference to the character narrator's feelings and thoughts by the use of 'verba sentiendi'.[52] (A term used by Uspensky, meaning words denoting feelings, thoughts and perceptions, primary signals of a subjective point of view.) In this writing, author's ideology is more prominent.

External perspective, Type 'C' — The narration is purely from an external point of view, there is no depiction of private feelings or emotions.

External perspective, Type 'D' — A single person/character controls the telling. The narrator may use first person pronouns with explicit modality and has definite views on the world.

Type A and B internal perspective combined result in — Free Indirect Discourse. This kind of writing combines character's subjective feelings with authorial commentary about the character's inner state. In such writings the author juxtaposes two sets of values.

Anita Desai's world is a world of subjective reality. She deals with 'primordial patterns of human experience'.[53]

As Usha Bande observes, "Through an artistic way of projecting life as it is — chequered emotionally as well as spiritually — Anita Desai shows the ability of her narrative art to maintain contact with life".[54]

Maya, in *Cry the Peacock*, Nirode, Amla, Monisha, in *Voices in the City*, Sita, in *Where Shall We Go This Summer*, Bim, in *Clear Light of Day*, Adit and Dev in *Bye-Bye Black Bird*, Deven, in *In Custody*, all are engaged in search of meaning of life, of understanding life, not concerned with the immediate problems of bread and butter but involved with the abstract human condition of love, hate, attachment and detachment.

The stance taken in these novels is that of third person subjective perspective and hence these novels combine a multiplicity of values.

As Freidman observes, "Every (modern) multivalent novel partakes of two determining characteristics (1) a self-conscious awareness of itself as artifact, as product, and (2) a counter pointing of conflicting ethical stances, a process in which one or more protagonists participate or serve as object".[55]

From the spatio temporal point of view, the novels of Anita Desai give the impression of slow motion pictures with sharpness and perspicacity. The movement is in full control by the recurring monologues and implicit dialogue very frequent in these novels. Disruptions in the natural flow of time can be marked in almost all the novels except, *A Village by the Sea*.

In the words of Friedman, "We follow not only the actions of the past but also the mind of the protagonist narrator as it seeks to recapture and depict, and therefore create, the past in the image of the present".[56]

The narrator takes a vantage point from which the characters are viewed clearly with the vivid physical background of flora and fauna, the earth and the sky, and if it happens to be a city, as in the *Voices in the City*, the entire gamut of the teeming millions, the throbbing, pulsating life around the protagonists is considered essential for depicting their various moods and reactions and yet the locus is the inner world of feelings and thoughts of these individuals.

The progression of time is more marked in *Bye-Bye Black Bird, In Custody*, and *A Village by the Sea*. In the latter two the effect of locomotion is more pronounced as the scenes change places. Hari moves from village to city and back to village and Deven keeps shuttling between Mirpore and Delhi. The other novels are more or less static in nature in this regard. In *Cry the Peacock*, the action is limited mostly to Maya's house, in *Voices in the City*, the city of Calcutta, in *Clear Light of Day*, it is the old house in Delhi, in *Where Shall We Go This Summer*, the island of Manori, in *Fire on the Mountain*, Carignano.

The ideological stance outwardly varying in different novels has certain common features. All the novels of Anita Desai are based on multiplicity of values, which are often conflicting with each other and are placed in a complex and ironic juxtaposition to each other. For *e.g.*, Maya and Gautam represent two different value systems. If Maya is all attached to life Gautam is the epitome of detachment. Nirode seeks to detach himself from family ties and property, Monisha can only lament about the lack of communication between her and her husband, for whom being a good provider is all that is required of a good husband. Amla on her part seeks the meaning of attachment and union of souls and is disillusioned to find fresh substitute motives for living and caring. Monisha fails in her quest and Nirode compromises with life in his own way.

Sita is another character engaged in a search for suitable ways of supporting creation. Juxtaposed with her are her father and husband who never made an issue of the normal process of creation but supported it in their own way.

Bim and Raja in, *Clear Light of Day*, wish to be hero and heroine when they grow up, while Tara was content to be happy with the love and security of human contact and the natural life process of becoming a wife and mother. Raja ends up as a property dealer, alienated from the family, and Bim an aging spinster full of bitterness and regret. Tara alone retains her balance and normalcy and is the medium of bringing about reconciliation and understanding between the alienated brother and sister.

Raka, Nanda Kaul and Ila Das represent three sets of values contrasted in the novel, *Fire on the Mountain.* Nanda Kaul is a recluse by pretence. Raka a recluse by choice and Ila Das a recluse by circumstance. All three trying to cope with life in the best manner possible.

Bye-Bye Black Bird, poses the problem of choice between flesh and spirit. The affluence and indifference of England opposed to the poverty, warmth and respect one gets at home in India, is the subject of choice for Dev and Adit. The tables are turned overnight with their visit to the English countryside. The author impartially describes the choice made by the two friends. Dev opts for England and Adit wants to return to India after savouring English life to the full.

For Sarah the choice to be made is between her old life and new life. For her the soul of living is not being on a piece of ground called England or India, but supporting the new life extended to her by her marriage to Adit.

Deven Sharma in *In Custody*, is a slave of a set of values which he respects temperamentally and which are in direct clash with his friend's — Murad. Gentle, trusting, self-respecting, Deven Sharma is a failure in life because he lacks practical sense and courage to assert himself. He works for Murad without payment, approaches Nur out of hero-worship, consents to the purchase of a second-hand tape-recorder, takes the help of students knowing fully well the implications and entertains letters from Nur out of sheer decency. These clashing values have forever been an enigma for man and will always continue to be so.

A Village by the Sea, does not overtly display any clash of values as such but directly describes the suffering and misery associated with a lack of responsibility in whatever form it may be. Hari's father unconcerned about the family, being a habitual drinker is responsible for the miseries and woes of the family. Later the same responsibility shouldered by Hari, and a reformation in the father, restore health and happiness to the family.

Besides the above personal values the novels display social values. The values of the Indian milieu described in the novels, dominate.

Indian community is by and large theistic. A belief in Almighty and different forms of worship are an integral part of Indian life even today. References to religion and worship are found in *Cry the Peacock*, in the form of excerpts from the *Gita*, *Voices in the City*, again refers to the *Gita* and explains the nature of *Goddess Kali*, *Fire on the Mountain*, refers to the Buddhist text, *The Pillow Book of Sei Shonagon*, *Where Shall We Go This Summer*?, has descriptions of prayer meetings and hour of worship at Manori, *Clear Light of Day*, does not refer to holy books or worship, but is full of quotations from poems suggesting a divine presence (*Clear Light of Day*, p. 100). *A Village by the Sea*, begins and ends with the reference to 'the three sacred rocks'.

Male female roles and relationships also reveal the Indian social values. As a necessity, communication or passionate attachment between husband and wife is not considered a must for marital harmony. We have the example of Maya and Gautam, Monisha and Jiban, Deven and Sarla, Sita and Raman. A woman if she is married should consider herself fortunate enough. A proof of her womanhood is her child bearing faculty. Both Maya and Monisha being childless are subjected to social derision and develop guilt feelings.

Indian male has always a dominating role to play and feels little responsible for the satisfaction of emotional needs of their wives or other women of the family. Even Adit living in England subjects Sarah to his tantrums. Hari's father in *A Village by the Sea*, is quite oblivious of his duty towards the family. The Vice Chancellor husband of Nanda Kaul feels unconcerned about his wife's needs and is content to live in his own paradise. Maya's story begins and ends with emotional starvation. Raja in *Clear Light of Day*, feels little concerned about the affectionate attention Bim demands.

Another noticeable contrast in values is drawn between the uneducated family women and the educated, self-reliant young women. Monisha decries Bengali women.

> 'I can imagine what she's like one of those vast, soft, masses-of-rice. Bengali women with a bunch of keys at her waist and nothing in her head but a reckoning of the stores in her pantry, and nothing in her heart but a stupid sense of injury and affront.'
>
> (*Voices in the City*, p. 81)

Opposed to these stupid women is the confidence and self-assurance of Amla, who represents the educated, enlightened womanhood of Indian cities today.

> 'I've heaps of ideas — I wonder if I'll get the chance to use them, as a commercial artist.'
>
> (*Voices in the City*, p. 154)

Social hypocrisy is another favourite topic of discussion for Anita Desai. The gap between appearance and reality surfaces in almost all her major novels. The worst part of it that in the Indian society it does not evoke social derision but has a calm acceptance.

Judgements and beliefs pertaining to the above are directly expressed by various modal structures including modal adverbs, sentence adverbs evaluative adjectives and generic sentences. The examples are not difficult to find.

Generic sentences with evaluative adjectives

> "Lives spent in waiting for nothing, waiting on men *self-centred* and *indifferent* and hungry and *demanding* and critical, waiting for death and dying misunderstood, *always* behind bars, these *terrifying* black bars that shut us in, in the old houses, in the old city."
>
> (*Voices in the City*, p. 120)

> "Gautam's reaction was *exactly* what I *might* have *predicted*, *had I thought* before speaking."
>
> (*Cry the Peacock*, p. 40)

A single sentence like the above contains a modal adverb, *exactly*, a modal auxiliary, *might*, a verb of prediction *predicted*, and another verb group denoting evaluation *had I thought*.

Psychological and Perceptual Point of View

Anita Desai's writing gains in depth and intensity mainly due to her psychological perspective. The various kinds of discourse at different levels is a result of the combination of internal and external perspectives.

An example of internal narration *Type A*, in which the narration is from the point of view of a character's consciousness is given below :

> "And then Gautam made a mistake — his last, decisive one. In talking, gesturing, he moved in front of me, thus coming between me and the worshipped moon, his figure an ugly crooked grey shadow that transgressed its sorrowing chastity 'Gautam' ! 'I screamed in fury, and thrust out my arms towards him, out at him, into him and past him saw him fall then, pass through'."
>
> (*Cry the Peacock*, p. 208)

Here in this passage, the first person variant is distinguished deictically by the use of first person singular pronouns. The judgements and opinions of Maya are foregrounded. She calls Gautam's step 'a decisive mistake'. There is a reference to character/narrator's feelings and thoughts. *Worshipped moon*, *his ugly figure*, *Crooked grey shadow*, and *sorrowing chastity*, indicate that. The choices of diction also indicate Maya as a certain psychological type.

Internal perspective *Type B* is based consistently on third person narration by an omniscient author who claims knowledge of the character's ideas, motives and feelings.

Example — 'Tara collected a bunch of velvet brown and purple pansies in the garden to take to school next day. But next day Miss Singh was gone. She had left with her bags, without a word, without a 'good bye' to a single girl, not even to Tara who stood at the open door of her room, rolling the bunch of pansies with their wide-eyed step-child faces. Tara was hurt, offended.'[57]

In this passage, prominence is given to the mental processes, feelings and perceptions of Tara. Her intentions, emotions and thoughts are highlighted.

There is no dearth of neutral, impersonal descriptions, conforming to *Type C* of Fowler's categories, in the writings of Anita Desai. An example :

> 'By the time the sun was up, turning the dull sea into peacock blue and emerald green and lighting up the city of Bombay on the far shore like a white castle made of sand or salt blinding against the hot blue sky, all the boats had been loaded and were setting out like a shoal of dolphins over the waves.'[58]
>
> (*A Village by the Sea*, p. 72)

The passage gives the impression of complete objectivity because action verbs and physical states are foregrounded. We have verb/participles, ***turning***, ***lighting***, ***blending***, ***loaded***, ***setting***, depicting actions and two similes *like a white castle made of sand*, and *like a shoal of dolphins*, creating word pictures of physical objects and beings. There is complete absence of modals and words of feelings.

Anita Desai's powers of description resulting in shifts of perspective are limitless. An example of Fowler's *Type D* perspective in which the narrator is highlighted and the impression of a narrator controlling the story who has definite views on the world at large (announced in generic sentences) is created.

Example : I am accused of theft.

> 'These pettiest of people. They regard me as meaner than they. They think me a thief. To be regarded so low, it is to be laid on a level lower than the common earth. I find that I am alone here. I find on this level that solitude that becomes me most naturally. I am willing to accept this status then, and to live here, a little beyond and below everyone else, in exile.
>
> (*Voices in the City*, p. 136)

The first person pronouns and explicit modality mark the passage. The author uses evaluative adjectives, *pettiest*, *meaner*, *low*, *lower*, *alone*, *most*, along with verbs of knowledge *find (2)*, *think, regard.* The narrator expresses generic views on men and women who accuse her (Monisha), of theft.

The above examples prove the multi-dimensional approach of Anita Desai, but her major writings are based on Free Indirect Discourse, *i.e.* a combination of *Type 'A'* and *Type 'B'* perspective.

Example :

> "Perhaps she ought to have refused to have her (Raka). Perhaps she ought to leave the house to Tara who needed shelter, a cave to crawl into and die. Perhaps, perhaps ....the alternatives were as many and as bothersome as flies. Nanda Kaul brushed them aside."
>
> (*Fire on the Mountain*, p. 103)

In the above passage the character's subjective feelings given in *Type A* narration are interwoven with and framed by the author's account of the character's inner state (Type B). The author juxtaposes two sets of values. Nanda Kaul wishes to leave the house to Raka but then thinks of Tara, her mother. The character is distanced from the reader and hence a critique of her (character's) views is possible without direct judgement.

The novels of Anita Desai considered under different subheadings in this chapter afford a wide spectrum of narrative perspectives. They are multivalent in their approach as Alan Warren Friedman says, 'almost invariably self-conscious and pluralistic, because they are simultaneously both a series of discrete parts and a unity and necessarily create and define a context, a pattern for themselves'.[59]

The discussion in the preceding pages is evidence enough that the understanding of prose fiction, like other literary works is aided through objective analysis. To conclude with the words of Wayne Booth :

"Narration is an art not a science, but this does not mean that we are necessarily doomed to fail when we attempt to formulate principles about it. There are systematic elements in every art and criticism of fiction can never avoid the responsibility of trying to explain technical successes and failures, by reference to general principles."[60]

REFERENCES

1. Geoffery N. Leech and Michael H. Short, *Style in Fiction* (London : Longman, 1981), p. 209.
2. Wayne C. Booth, *The Rhetoric of Fiction* (Chicago : Chicago University Press, 1961), Preface.
3. David Lodge, *Language of Fiction* (London : Routledge and Kegan Paul, 1966), p. 147.
4. Henry James, *Selected Literary Criticism Henry James*, ed. Morris Shapira (New York : McGraw Hill Paperbacks, 1965), p. 65.
5. Leech and Short, pp. 178-180.
6. Darshan Singh Maini, "Anita Desai's Novels : An Evaluation", in *Perspectives on Anita Desai*, ed. R.K. Shrivastava (Ghaziabad : Vimal Prakashan, 1984), p. 125.
7. Booth, p. 127.
8. Leech and Short, p. 209.
9. *Ibid.*, p. 259.
10. Booth, p. 73.
11. *Ibid.*, p. 74.
12. Darshan Singh Maini, 'Anita Desai's Novels : An Evaluation", in *Perspectives on Anita Desai*, ed. R.K. Shrivastava (Ghaziabad : Vimal Prakashan, 1984), p. 120.
13. Anita Desai, *Cry the Peacock* (1963, Delhi : Vision Books, 1983), pp. 102-3.
14. H.M. Williams, *Indo-Anglian Literature 1800-1970 : A Survey* (New Delhi : Orient Longman Ltd., 1976), p. 89.
15. R.S. Sharma, *Anita Desai* (Liverpool : Lucas Publications, 1981), p. 92.
16. *Ibid.*, pp. 130-31.
17. Anita Desai, *Fire on the Mountain* (Middlesex : Penguin Books, 1977), pp. 3-5.
18. Booth, p. 49.
19. Dorothea Krook, "Intentions and Intentions, The Problem of intention and Henry James' Turn of the screw", in *The Theory of the Novel*, ed. John Halperin (New York : Oxford University Press, 1974), p. 353.
20. Booth, p. 42.
21. Leech and Short, p. 265.
22. Booth, p. 212.
23. Miriam Allott, *Novelists on the Novel* (London : Routledge and Kegan Paul, 1959), p. 188.
24. *Ibid.*, p. 260.

25. Henry James, "Preface to the Ambassadors", in *Novelists on the Novel*, ed. Miriam Allott (London : Routledge and Kegan Paul, 1959), p. 261.
26. *Ibid.*, p. 188.
27. Booth, p. 45.
28. Miriam Allott, p. 265.
29. Miriam Allott, p. 197.
30. Percy Lubbock, *The Art of Fiction* (London : 1921), p. 62.
31. Booth, p. 174.
32. Roger Fowler, *Linguistic Criticism* (New York : Oxford University Press, 1986), pp. 118-20.
33. Anita Desai, *Where Shall We Go This Summer?* (Delhi : Orient Paperbacks, 1975), p. 89.
34. Leech and Short, p. 265.
35. *Ibid.*, p. 280.
36. Booth, p. 125.
37. *Ibid.*, pp. 155-56.
38. Leech and Short, p. 283.
39. Quoted from, *The Theory of the Novel*, ed. John Halperin (New York : Oxford University, 1974), p. 297.
40. *Ibid.*, p. 298.
41. Walter F. Wright, "Tone in Fiction", in *The Theory of the Novel*, ed. John Halperin (New York : Oxford University Press, 1974), pp. 300-4.
42. Anita Desai, *Voices in the City* (New Delhi : Orient Paperbacks, 1965), p. 5.
43. Leech and Short, p. 287.
44. *Ibid.*, p. 291.
45. Fowler, p. 104.
46. Roger Fowler, p. 106.
47. Anita Desai, *In Custody* (London : Penguin Books, 1984), p. 10.
48. Leech and Short, p. 174.
49. *Ibid.*, p. 174.
50. Roger Fowler, p. 127.
51. *Ibid.*, p. 134.
52. Boris Uspensky, *A Poetics of Composition*, trans. Zavarin and Suzan Wittig (Berkley : University of California Press, 1973).
53. Alan Warren Friedman, "The Modern Multivalent Novel" in *The Theory of the Novel*, ed. John Halperin (New York : Oxford University Press, 1974), p. 130.

54. Usha Bande, *The Novels of Anita Desai* (New Delhi : Prestige Books, 1988), p. 175.
55. Alan Warren Friedman, p. 137.
56. *Ibid.*, p. 133.
57. Anita Desai, *Clear Light of Day* (New Delhi : Allied Publishers, 1980), p. 129.
58. Anita Desai, *A Village by the Sea* (New Delhi : Allied Publishers, 1983), p. 72.
59. Alan Warren Friedman, p. 122.
60. Booth, p. 164.

5

CONCLUSION

> "All stylistic analysis is ultimately based on the matching of a text against a contextually related norm. Such norms may be explicitly circumscribed, or they may remain implicitly embedded in the past experience of a speaker, writer or literary critic."[1]
>
> *—Nils Eric Enkvist*

> "Style at its best is the product of a worthwhile mind and sensibility expressing itself in terms appropriate to a given subject, and that style, when appropriate, is a part of the meaning. Style is also the expression of a motivating spirit and therefore of an era or a culture."[2]
>
> *—William Van O'Connor*

From the stand point of prevailing trends in stylistics, the novels of Anita Desai reveal marked characteristics of all three types of style studies, *i.e.*, "those that treat style as a norm, those that emphasise recurrence or convergence of textual patterns, and those that concentrate on a particular exploitation of a grammar of possibilities.

Desai's deviant use of lexis foregrounds some expression or the other very frequently, in fact some critics consider them too frequent. Marked contextual patterns in smaller units like sentences and paragraphs are part of the special design on which each work is framed. Conventional plots are replaced by carefully wrought artistic plans, befitting the underlying idea. Her varied application of different grammatical categories and devices according to the requirements of context, and explicit and implicit cohesive devices make her language natural, fluent and striking. The end product is a happy combination of conceptual and non-conceptual deviance. As a result of all the above characteristics, her novels can be placed in Bacon's third category *i.e.*, 'those which are to be chewed and digested'.

Every star has its own orbit, and Anita Desai too has her own circle of reading public. All writing in general is a means of communication between the author and the reader, how far the author succeeds in this task depends on their mutual apprehension of reality. If the author's conception and presentation coincides with the expectations of the reader, or if the author delights the reader by giving him fresh "objective correlatives", as Eliot would say, a rapport between the author and reader is established.

Anita Desai's approach is different from the conventional fiction. Her work reveals strong affinities with modern fiction.

> "The realism of Lewis and Dreiser; the attempt to capture the feelings that border and merge with the unconscious and the currents of sensation passing between characters, as in Lawrence; the effort to bring into some kind of focus the hetrogenous complexity of ideas, feelings and impressions in individual minds, as in Joyce and Virginia Woolf, and the concern to bring into juxtaposition multiple points of view, as in Gide and Huxley. Each of these novelists has attempted to find a norm whereby he might appropriately objectify or dramatize his understanding of our time".[3]

Anita Desai focuses her attention on the fundamental problems of existence, rather than on the attainment of easy goals in life which occupy most of us. Her greatest asset is her language and the novelty of approach is in her technique. As Mark Schorer remarks, "The resources of a language are a part of technique of fiction — language used to create a certain texture and tone, which in themselves state and define themes and meanings."[4] Meenakshi Mukerjee has aptly remarked, "Anita Desai is a rare example of an Indo-Anglian writer who achieves the difficult task of bending English Language to her purpose without either a self-conscious attempt at sounding Indian or seeking the anonymous elegance of public school English".[5]

Desai's poetic vision is manifest in every word and phrase that she selects. The analysis of the beginning pages of her eight novels confirms the truth of the statement. Every single page is representative of her penetrating vision justifying her claim as a lyrical novelist. "A prose poem", Ralph Freedman say, "is an ideal novel, because it can contract the novel's substance into one or two pages, it manages to contain in its small volume in a state of 'meat' the power of the novel which suppresses all the analytical passages and descriptive involvements".[6] It is noteworthy that the novels of Anita Desai are short and therefore Prof. Maini[7] considers them 'novelles' rather than novels.

A world of images is another special feature of these novels based on 'subjective objectivity' *i.e.*, the subjective experiences of the protagonists are objectified through concrete images. Anita Desai has often been criticised for excessive imagery, but a careful study reveals that the images in these novels "produce a surprise effect and a kind of inverted expressiveness".[8] The balanced use of concrete and abstract nouns, the dynamic and stative verbs, gradable and non-gradable adjectives, the deft use of adjuncts, conjuncts and disjuncts and the preference for monosyllabic words for polysyllabic words indicating a judicious mixture of Saxon and Latin words all attest to her ability to convert the subjective into objective.

The technique of 'Free Indirect Discourse', which has been freely used in these novels is a distinctive feature of psychological novels. Psychological analysis and concern with primeval issues, however valuable to our understanding of life are certainly not the choice of many a reader who picks up a work of literary art, and especially a novel more for entertainment, rather than to be lured into thinking about serious problems of life. Incidentally these problems are the very theme of modern fiction. Irwing Howe writes :

> "A modernist culture is committed to the view that the human lot is inescapably problematic : Problems to be sure have been noticed at all times, but in a modernist culture, the problematic as a style of existence and enquiry becomes imperious : men learn to find comfort in their wounds, Nietzsche says : Truth has never hung on the arms of the absolute."[9]

Anita Desai like Virginia Woolf reveals the twentieth century "preoccupation with flux and the shifting centres of personal identity, and hence has tried to emphasise a personal, subjective sense of reality".[10]

To conclude a stylistic study on these lines may perhaps seem unjustified, but as Booth remarks,

> "When human actions are formed to make an art-work the form that is made can never be divorced from the human meanings, including the moral judgements, that are implicit whenever human beings act, and nothing the writer does can be finally understood in isolation from his effort to make it all accessible to someone else, his peers, himself, an imagined reader, his audience.
>
> ...The author makes his readers, if he makes them well — that is makes them see what they have never seen before, moves them to a new order of perception and experience together — he finds his reward in the peers he has created."[11]

The novel outlook on life presented by Anita Desai is due to the force of her expression and ideology both. We sympathize with Maya, Nirode, Monisha, Nanda Kaul, Raka, Sita, Deven, Adit, Dev, Bim, Hari, Lila and others, because they are in search of a deeper, fuller meaning of life, and through the power of her words, Anita Desai has made them reverberate the very impulses we feel within ourselves.

REFERENCES

1. Nils Eric Enkvist, 'On Defining Style' in *Linguistics and Style*, ed. John Spencer (London : Oxford University Press, 1964), p. 54.
2. William Van O'Connor, "The Novel in our Time" in *Forms of Modern Fiction*, ed. William Van O'Connor (1959, rpt.; Bloomington : Indiana University Press, 1964), p. 7.
3. William Van O'Connor, p. 2.
4. Mark Schorer, 'Technique as Discovery', in *Forms of Modern Fiction*, ed. William Van O'Connor, p. 9.
5. Meenakshi Mukerjee, *Twice Born Fiction* (New Delhi : Arnold Heinmann, 1974), pp. 190-91.
6. Ralph Freedman, *The Lyrical Novel* (Princeton : Princeton University Press, 1963), p. 37.
7. Darshan Singh Maini, 'Anita Desai's Novels : An Evaluation', in *Perspectives on Anita Desai*, ed. R.K. Shrivastava (Ghaziabad : Vimal Prakashan, 1984), p. 120.
8. Stephen Ullman, *Style in French Novel* (Oxford : Basil Blackwell, 1964), p. 216.

9. Irwing Howe, "The Idea of the Modern", in *The Idea of the Modern in Literature and Arts*, ed. Irwing Howe (New York : Horizon Press, 1967), pp. 18-19.
10. William Van O'Connor, p. 4.
11. Wayne C. Booth, *The Rhetoric of Fiction* (1961; rpt.; Chicago : University of Chicago Press, 1963), pp. 397-98.

APPENDIX

TABLE I

Numerical Data used in Chapter 2

CATEGORIES	CRY THE THE PEACOCK 1963	VOICES IN THE CITY 1965	BYE-BYE BLACK BIRD 1971	WHERE SHALL WE GO THIS SUMMER? 1975	FIRE ON THE MOUNTAIN 1977	CLEAR LIGHT OF DAY 1980	A VILLAGE BY THE SEA 1982	IN CUSTODY 1984
No. of graphological words in the extract	514	516	501	520	490	526	492	513
No. of graphological sentences	25	25	11	30	22	17	22	33
No. of words per sentence	20.56	20.68	45.54	17.33	22.27	30.94	22.36	15.63

TABLE II

Major Word Classes

CATEGORIES	CRY THE THE PEACOCK 1963	VOICES IN THE CITY 1965	BYE-BYE BLACK BIRD 1971	WHERE SHALL WE GO THIS SUMMER? 1975	FIRE ON THE MOUNTAIN 1977	CLEAR LIGHT OF DAY 1980	A VILLAGE BY THE SEA 1982	IN CUSTODY 1984
NOUNS — Total No.	80	99	78	91	83	80	89	100
Concrete	75	75	58	71	63	66	81	82
Abstract	05	24	15	15	16	13	07	14
Proper	00	03	05	06	04	01	01	04
MAIN VERBS — Total No.	76	61	58	57	49	60	41	73
Transitive	66	23	29	29	35	53	23	66
Intransitive	08	23	29	28	14	07	18	10
ADJECTIVES	23	18	15	50	21	19	24	16
ADVERBS	31	16	25	20	14	21	32	14
ARTICLES — Total No.	39	29	28	26	29	44	31	31
Definite	29	11	21	18	23	35	24	13
Indefinite	11	18	07	08	06	09	07	08

BIBLIOGRAPHY

I. PRIMARY SOURCES

Anita Desai Works

(i) Novels

Cry the Peacock. London : Peter Owen, 1963. Calcutta : Rupa Publishers, 1964. Delhi : Orient Paperbacks, 1980. Delhi : Vision Books, 1983.

Tipatul Panulai. Rumania : Colectia Meridiane, 1966 (in Rumanian).

Voices in the City. London : Peter Owen, 1965. Delhi : Hind Pocket Books, 1971. Orient Paperbacks, 1965.

Bye-Bye Black Bird. Delhi : Hind Pocket Books, 1971. Delhi : Vision Books, 1985.

Where Shall We Go This Summer? Delhi : Vikas Publishing House, 1975. Delhi : Orient Paperbacks, 1982.

Fire on the Mountain. London : William Heinemann, 1978. New York : Harper and Row, 1977. Delhi : Allied, 1977. Sweden : Trivi, 1980. Harmondsworth : King Penguin, 1983.

Clear Light of Day. London : William Heinemann, 1980. New York : Harper and Row, 1980. New Delhi : Allied, 1980. Harmondsworth : King Penguin, 1983.

In Custody. London : William Heinemann, 1984.

Baumgartner's Bombay. London : William Heinemann, 1988.

(ii) For Children

The Peacock Garden. Bombay : India Book House, 1974. London : William Heinemann, 1979.

Cat on a Houseboat. Bombay : Orient Longman, 1976.

Village by the Sea. London : William Heinemann, 1982. Delhi : Allied, 1983.

(iii) Short Stories

Games at Twilight. London : William Heinemann, 1978. Bombay : Allied, 1978. New York : Harper and Row, 1980. Sweden : Trivi, 1980. Harmondsworth : Penguin, 1982. The anthology includes "Pineapple Cake," "Games at Twilight," "Private Tuition by Mr. Bose," "Studies in the Park," "Surface Texture," "Sale," "The Accompanist," "A Devoted Son," "The Farewell Party," "Pigeons at Daybreak," "Scholar and Gypsy."

(iv) Uncollected Short Stories

"Circus Cat, Alley Cat." Delhi : *Thought*, 1957. Collected in M.C. Gabriel and Gwen Gabriel, eds., *A Selection of Modern Indian Short Stories*. Delhi : Sidhartha, 1968, pp. 95-98.

"How Gentle is the Mist." *The Illustrated Weekly of India*, 1958.

"Tea with the Maharani." *Envoy*, 4 (January-February 1959).

"Grand Mother." *Writers Workshop Miscellany*, 1 (August 1960).

"An Examination." *Writers Workshop Miscellany*, 3 (1960).

"Ghost House." *Quest* (Jan.-March, 1961).

"Mr. Bose's Private Bliss." *Envoy*, 6 (May-June 1961).

"Private Tuition by Mr. Bose." Delhi : *Indian Literature*, 1970.

"To Sell a Picture." *Writers Workshop Miscellany*, 6 (1961).

"Descent from the Roof-top." *The Illustrated Weekly of India*, 91, 4 Jan. 1970, pp. 36-39.

"Surface Texture." *Femina*, 1974.

"The Accompanist." *Quest*, 1975.

(v) Essays, Articles, Reviews

"Calcutta Kaleidoscope." *The Illustrated Weekly of India*, 1958.

"Gangtok." London : Enovy, 1959.

"A Kulu Christmas." London : Envoy, 1959.

"Pilgrimage." *The Illustrated Weekly of India*, 1966.

"Women Writers." Quest, No. 65, April-June 1970, pp. 39-43.

"The Indian Writers' Problems." *The Literary Criterion*, 12 (Summer, 1975), pp. 26-36. Rpt. in *Explorations in Modern Indo-English Fiction*, ed. R.K. Dhawan. New Delhi : Bahri, 1982.

"Timid Movement of a Wing." *The Indian Literary Review* (August 1978), pp. 11-13.

"Within and Without Tradition." ACLALS *Newsletter*, 5 April 1979, pp. 5-21.

"Memoirs of a Mendicant Professor." (A Review) *Quest*, 66 (July-Sept. 1970).

"Out of the Shadows." *Indian Express*, June 10, 1984.

(vi) Interviews/Questionnaire

In Custody. London : William Heinemann, 1984.

"Reply to the Questionnaire." *Kakatiya Journal of English Studies*, 3 (1978), pp.1-6.

"An Interview with Anita Desai," by Yashodhara Dalmia. *The Times of India*, 29 April 1979.

"Anita Desai : Interviewed," by Jasbir Jain. *Rajasthan University Studies in English*, 12 (1979), pp. 61-69.

"An Interview with Anita Desai," by Atma Ram. *World Literature Written in English*, 16, No. 1 (November 1977), pp. 95-104. Reprinted in *Interviews with Indian English Writers*. Atma Ram. Calcutta : Writers Workshop, 1983.

"Tremendous Changes." Interview by Sunil Seth. *India Today*, December 1-15, 1980.

"Anita Desai at Work : An Interview," by Ramesh K. Srivastava. *Perspectives on Anita Desai*, ed. Ramesh K. Srivastava. Ghaziabad : Vimal, 1984.

"It's Fatal to Write with an Audience in Mind," An Interview by Ketaki Sheth, Imprint (June 1984).

II. SECONDARY SOURCES

(i) *Critical Material on Anita Desai*

(a) Books/Anthologies

Bande, Usha. *The Novels of Anita Desai*, New Delhi : Prestige Books, 1988.

Belliappa, Meena. Anita Desai : A Study of Her Fiction. Calcutta : Writers Workshop, 1971.

Jain, Jasbir. *Stairs to the Attic : The Novels of Anita Desai*, Jaipur : Printwell, 1987.

Prasad, Madhusudan. *Anita Desai : The Novelist.* Allahabad : New Horizon, 1981.

Rao, B. Ramachandra. *The Novels of Anita Desai.* New Delhi : Kalyani, 1977.

Sharma, R.S. *Anita Desai.* New Delhi : Arnold Heinemann, 1981.

Shrivastava, Ramesh K., ed. *Perspectives on Anita Desai.* Ghaziabad : Vimal, 1984.

(b) Articles/Essays/Reviews

Acharya, Shanta. "Problems of the Self in the Novels of Anita Desai." *Explorations in Modern Indo-English Fiction*, ed. R.K. Dhawan. New Delhi : Bahri, 1982, pp. 236-54.

Alcock, Peter. "Rope, Serpent, Fire : The Recent Fiction of Anita Desai." *Journal of Indian Writing in English*, Vol. IX, No. 1, Jan. 81, pp. 15-34.

Asnani, Shyam M. "Anita Desai's Fiction : A New Dimension." *Indian Literature*, 24, 2. March-April 1981, pp. 44-54.

———. "Theme of Withdrawal and Loneliness in Anita Desai's *Fire on the Mountain*." *Journal of Indian Writing in English*, Vol. IX, No. 1, Jan. 81, pp. 81-92.

———. "Anita Desai : The Novelist with Unique Personal Vision." Contemporary Indian Thought, Vol. 14, No. 1, Jan.-March 1974, pp. 6-9, 16-21.

Bannerjee, Purabi. "Bookworm's Progress." *Statesman*, 10 April 1983.

Daftry, Nayana. "Review of *Cry the Peacock*." *Quest*, Vol. 10, No. 1, Winter, 1983, p. 50.

Daruwalla, Keki N. "Built on a Non-issue." Review of *In Custody. The Hindustan Times*, 13 Jan. 1985.

Dua, M.R. "Anita Desai." *Femina*, 4 Jan. 1974, p. 25.

Dubashi, Jagannath. "*The Village by the Sea* : An Indian Family Story : Review." *India Today*, 15 April 1983.

Dult, Charmazel. "Past and Present : A Journey to Confrontation." *Journal of Indian Writing in English*, Vol. IX, No. 1, 1981, pp. 67-73.

Gabriele, A. "Anita Desai's *Fire on the Mountain*. A Review." *Times Literary Supplement*, 17 June 1977, p. 721.

———. "Dreams in Old Delhi." *Times Literary Supplement*, 5, Sept. 1980, p. 948.

Ganguli, Chandra. "Fire on the Mountain : An Analysis." Critical Quarterly, 6 (Dec. 1981), pp. 43-44.

Glendinning, Victoria. "Mood Indigo," Review of *Games at Twilight and Other Stories*. *Times Literary Supplement*, 1978, p. 973.

Hashima, A. "Review of *Clear Light of Day*." *International Fiction*, 1963, pp. 99-101.

Jain, Jasbir. "Anita Desai." *Indian English Novelists*, ed. Madhusudan Prasad. New Delhi : Sterling, 1982, pp. 23-50.

———. "The Use of Fantasy in Anita Desai's Novels." *Explorations in Modern Indo-English Fiction*, ed. R.K. Dhawan. New Delhi : Bahri, 1982, pp. 227-37.

Jamkhandi, Sudhakar Ratnakar. "Artistic Effects of the Shifts in Point of View in Anita Desai's *Cry the Peàcock*." *Journal of Indian Writing in English*, Vol. IX, No. 1, Jan. 81, pp. 35-46.

———. "Old Delhi Revisited : Anita Desai's *Clear Light of Day*," *Commonwealth Fiction*, ed. R.K. Dhawan. Classical : 1988, Vol. I, pp. 245-53.

Krishna, Francine E. "A Lulled Life." Review of *Where Shall We Go This Summer*? *Quest*, No. 99, Jan.-Feb. 1976, pp. 90-91.

———. "Anita Desai : *Fire on the Mountain*," *Indian Literature*, Vol. 25, No. 5, Sept.-Oct. 1982, pp. 58-69.

Krishnaswamy, Shantha. "Anita Desai — The Sexist Nature of Sanity." *The Woman in Indian Fiction in English* (1950-80). New Delhi : Ashish Publishing House. 1982.

Kumar, Shiv K. "The Fiction of Anita Desai : Another View." *The Humanities Review*, 3, July-December 1981, pp. 43-46.

Lal, P. "Review of *Voices in the City*." *Littcrit*, Vol. 2, No. 2, Dec. 1976, pp. 51-53.

———. "Review of *Cry, the Peacock*." *Nagpur Times*, 15 Dec. 1968.

———. "Review of *Cry the Peacock*." *Times Literary Supplement*, No. 3, 182, Friday, 22 Feb. 1963.

Maini, D.S. "Achievement of Anita Desai." *Indo-English Literature*, ed. K.K. Sharma. Ghaziabad : Vimal, 1977, pp. 215-30.

———. "*Cry the Peacock as a Poetic Novel*." *English Literature* of the Past Fifty Years, 1917-67, ed. C.D. Narasimhaiah. Mysore : University of Mysore, 1970, pp. 225-34.

Malhotra, M.J. "Anita Desai : A Writer with a Promise." *Bridges of Literature*. Ajmer : Sunanda Publications, 1971, pp. 205-22.

Mukherjee, Meenakshi, "The Theme of Displacement in Anita Desai and Kamala Markandaya." *World Literature Written in English*, 17, No. 1 (April 1978), pp. 225-35.

———. Review of *Bye-Bye, Black Bird*. *Quest*, 75 (March-April 1972), pp. 96-99.

———. *Considerations*. New Delhi : Allied, 1977.

Pande, Mrinal. "Women Without Men." Review of *Fire on the Mountain*. *The Times of India*, 18 Dec. 1977, p. 1.

Prasad, Hari Mohan. "Sound or Sense : A Study of Anita Desai's *Bye-Bye, Black Bird*." *Journal of Indian Writing in English*, Vol. IX, No. 1, Jan. 1981, pp. 51-66.

Rao, A.V. Krishna. "*Village by the Sea* : A Review." *Journal of Indian Writing in English*, 2, No. 2, July 1983.

Rao, Vimala. "*Where Shall We Go This Summer*? An Analysis." *Commonwealth Quarterly*, Vol. 3, No. 9, Dec. 1978.

Ram, Atma. "Anita Desai." *Journal of Indian Writing in English*, 5, No. 2 (July 1977), pp. 39-42.

———. "*Where Shall We Go This Summer?*" *World Literature Written in English*, 15, No. 2, Nov. 1976, pp. 381-83.

———. "Anita Desai : Exploration of Inner Sensibility." *Perspective*, July 1978, pp. 54-55.

———. "Indians Slow to Recognise Talent in their Midst." *The Tribune*, 26 June 1977.

——. "A View of *Where Shall We Go This Summer?*" *The Journal of Indian Writing in English*, 9, No. 1, January 1981, pp. 74-80; rpt., Response : *Recent Revelations of Indian Fiction in English*, ed. Hari Mohan Prasad. Bareilly : Prakash Book Depot, 1983, pp. 241-48.

———. "Shiv K. Kumar and Anita Desai : New Dimension to Indian English Fiction." *Triveni*, Jan.-March 1984, pp. 32-37.

Rao, Shyamala B. "Women Writers in Indo-Anglian Fiction." *Century*, 26 Jan. 1972, pp. 25-34.

Ray, Karen. "*Clear Light of Day* : A Review." *Christian Science Monitor*, 28 Jan. 1981, p. 17.

Reuben, Elizabeth. "Anita Desai's *Fire on the Mountain.*" *World Literature Written in English*, 17, No. 1, April 1978, pp. 234-36.

Sethi, Sunil. "Pieces of the Past." Review of Anita Desai's *Clear Light of Day*. *India Today*, 5, No. 23, December 1-15, 1980, pp. 142-43.

Sharma, D.R. "Anita Desai." *The Tribune*, 2 April 1978.

Sharma, R.S. "Alienation, Accommodation and the Locale in Anita Desai's *Bye-Bye, Black Bird.*" *Literary Criterion*, Vol. 14, No. 4, 1979, pp. 31-49.

———. "Movement and Stillness in Anita Desai's *Fire on the Mountain.*" *Littcrit*, Vol. 4, No. 2, Dec. 1978, pp. 1-6.

———. "Mother and the City : Archetypes in Anita Desai's *Voices in the City.*" *Journal of Literary Studies*, Vol. 2, No. 2, Dec. 1979, pp. 57-77.

Shastri, N.R. "*Where Shall We Go This Summer?* : A Critical Study." *Osmania Journal of English Studies*, Vol. 17, 1981, pp. 83-103.

Singh, Brij Raj. "The Fiction of Anita Desai." *The Humanities Review*, 3, No. 2 (July-December 1981), pp. 40-43.

Singh, C.P. "The Visitor and the Exile : A Study in Anita Desai's *Bye-Bye, Black Bird*." *Response : Recent Revelations of Indian Fiction in English*, ed. Hari Mohan Prasad. Bareilly : Prakash Book Depot, 1983.

Singh, R.S. "Aloneness Alone : Anita Desai and Arun Joshi." *Indian Novel in English*. New Delhi : Arnold Heinemann, 1977, pp. 164-77.

Sivaramakrishna. "From Alienation to Mythic Acceptance : The Ordeal of Consciousness in Anita Desai's Fiction." *Kakatiya Journal of English Studies*, 3, No. 1, 1978, pp. 7-24.

Srivastava, Ramesh K. "*Voices of Artists in the City*." *Journal of Indian Writing in English*, Vol. IX, No. 1, Jan. 1981, pp. 47-57.

Sunwain, V.K. "Carignano — A Quiet Place." *Journal of Literary Studies*, 2, No. 2, Dec. 1979, pp. 79-92.

Vyas, B.O. "Vivid Voices of the Inner Kingdom." *Journal of Indian Writing in English*, Vol. IV, No. 1, Jan. 1981, pp. 1-14.

Weir, Ann Lowry. "The Illusion of Maya : Feminine consciousness in Anita Desai's *Cry, the Peacock*." *Journal of South Asian Literature*, 21, No. 2, Summer-Fall 1981, pp. 1-41.

(ii) *Critical Material on Language, Style, Stylistics and Fiction*

Aristotle, Horace, Longinus. *Classical Literary Criticism*. Middlesex : Penguin Books. 1987.

Allott, Miriam. *Novelists on the Novel*. London : Routledge and Kegan Paul. 1959.

Abraham, M.N. ed. *A Glossary of Literary Terms*. New York : Holt Rinehart and Winston. 1971.

Baugh, A.C. *A History of the English Language*. London : Routledge & Kegan Paul. 1959.

Booth, Wayne, C. *The Rhetoric of Fiction*. Chicago : Chicago University-Press. 1961.

Boulton, Marjorie. *The Anatomy of Prose*. London : Routledge and Kegan Paul. 1968.

Bahri, Hardev. *Definitional Dictionary of Linguistic Terms*. New Delhi : National. 1985.

Corder, S. Pit. *Introducing Applied Linguistics*. Middlesex, Penguin Education. 1973.

Dobree, Bonamy. *Modern Prose Style*. London : Oxford Clarendon Press. 1964.

Dey, Shushil Kumar. *Studies in the History of Sanskrit Poetics*. London : Luzac and Co. 1923.

Darbyshire, A.H. *A Grammar of Style*. London : Andre Deutsch. 1971.

Enkvist, N.E., Spencer, J., and Gregory, M.J. *Linguistics and Style*, Oxford UP. 1964.

Enkvist, N.E. *Linguistic Stylistics*. The Hague and Paris. Moulton. 1973.

———. 'On defining style', in Enkvist, N.E., Spencer, J., and Gregory, M.J. 1964. pp. 1-56.

Fowler, Roger. ed. *Essays on Style and Language*. London : University College. 1967.

——— *Linguistics and the Novel*. London : Methuen. 1977.

——— *Linguistic Criticism*. New York : Oxford UP. 1986.

Freedman, Ralph. *The Lyrical Novel*. Princeton : Princeton University Press. 1963.

Freeman, D.C. *Linguistics and Literary Style*, New York : Holt. 1970.

Frye, N. *The Anatomy of Criticism*. Princeton N.J., Princeton UP. 1957.

Forster, E.M. *Aspects of the Novel*. London : Edward Arnold. 1945.

Hough, Graham. *Style and Stylistics*. London : Routledge and Kegan Paul. 1969.

Halliday, M.A.K., and Hasan, R. *Cohesion in English*. London : Longmans. 1976.

Halliday, M.A.K., McIntosh, A. and Strevens, P. *Linguistic Sciences* and *Language Teaching*. 1964.

Halperin, John ed. *The Theory of the Novel*. New York : Oxford UP. 1974.

Howe, Irwing. *The Idea of the Modern in Literature and Art*. New York : Horizon Press. 1967.

Hockett, C.F. *A Course in Modern Linguistics*. New York : Macmillan. 1958.

Iyengar, K.R.S. *Indian Writings in English*. New Delhi : Sterling. 1962.

James, Henry. *Selected Literary Criticism*. ed. Morris Shapira. New York : McGraw. 1965.

Jones, D. *Every Man's English Pronouncing Dictionary*. Revised and ed. London : Gimson, A.C. and Dent.

Leech, G., *A Linguistic Guide to Poetry*. London : Longman. 1969.

——— *Semantics*. Harmondsworth : Penguin. 1974.

——— "This Bread I Break : Language and Interpretation.'' Review of English Literature, 6, 2, 66-75; rpt. in Freeman, D.C. ed. 1970, 119-28.

Leech, G.N., and Short, Michael, H. *Style in Fiction*. London & New York : Longman. 1981.

Lodge, David. *Language of Fiction*. London : Routledge and Kegan Paul. 1970. "Metaphor and Metonymy in Modern Fiction. *Critical Quarterly*, Vol. 17, No. 1. Spring 1975.

Lucas, F.L. *Style*. London : Cassell and Co. 1974.

Lubbock, Percy. *The Art of Fiction*. London. 1921.

Mukerjee, Meenakshi. *Twice Born Fiction*. New Delhi : Arnold Heinemann. 1974.

Mukarovsky, J. "Standard Language and Poetic Language," in Garvin, P.L. 1978, 17-30; rpt. Freeman, D.C. 1970. 258-78.

Murrey, J. Middleton *The Problem of Style*. London : Oxford UP. 1967.

O'Connor, William Van. *Forms of Modern Fiction*. Bloomington : Indiana University Press, 1974.

Quirk, R. and Greenbaum, S. *A Univeristy Grammar of English.* London : Longman. 1973.

Read, Herbert. *English Prose Style.* Ludhiana : Lyall Book Depot. 1968.

Robins, R.H. *A Short History of Linguistics.* London & New York : Longman. 1979.

Richards, I.A. *Practical Criticism.* London : Routledge and Kegan Paul. 1954.

Raghavan, V. *Some Aspects of Alankara Shastra.* Adyar : The Adyar Library. 1942.

Sebeok, T.A. ed. *Style in Language.* Cambridge, Mars., MIT Press. 1961.

Searle, J.R. *Speech Acts.* Cambridge Univ. Press. 1969.

Ullman, S. *Style in the French Novel.* London : Oxford UP. 1957.

——— *Meaning and Style.* Oxford : Blackwell. 1973.

Uspensky, Boris. *A Poetics of Composition.* Trans. Zavarin and Suzan Wiggig. Berkley : University of California Press, 1973.

Wellek, Rene, Warren, Austin. *Theory of Literature.* Middlesex : Penguin Books. 1973.

Warburog, J. *Some Aspects of Style* : The Teaching of English, Studies in Communication. 3 ed. Randolf Quirk & A.H. Smith. 1959.

Williams, H.M. *Indo-Anglian Literature.* 1800-1970. A Survey. New Delhi : Orient Longman. 1976.

Warner, Alan. *A Short Guide to English Style.* London : Oxford UP. 1961.

Index